THE HYBRID LEADER

Evolving, Adaptable, Unfinished

IRVING H. BUCHEN

Rowman & Littlefield Education
A division of

ROWMAN & LITTLEFIELD PUBLISHERS, INC.
Lanham • New York • Toronto • Plymouth, UK

Published by Rowman & Littlefield Education
A division of Rowman & Littlefield Publishers, Inc.
A wholly owned subsidiary of The Rowman & Littlefield Publishing Group, Inc.
4501 Forbes Boulevard, Suite 200, Lanham, Maryland 20706
http://www.rowmaneducation.com

Estover Road, Plymouth PL6 7PY, United Kingdom

British Library Cataloguing in Publication Information Available

Library of Congress Cataloging-in-Publication Data

Buchen, Irving H., 1930–
  The hybrid leader : evolving, adaptable, unfinished / Irving Buchen.
    p. cm.
  ISBN 978-1-60709-616-0 (cloth : alk. paper) — ISBN 978-1-60709-617-7 (pbk. : alk.
paper) — ISBN 978-1-60709-594-1 (electronic)
  1. Leadership. 2. Executive ability. 3. Intellect. I. Title.
  HD57.7.B834 2011
  658.4'092—dc23   2011019169

∞ ™ The paper used in this publication meets the minimum requirements of American
National Standard for Information Sciences—Permanence of Paper for Printed Library
Materials, ANSI/NISO Z39.48-1992. Printed in the United States of America

To Rabbi Devora:
A one-of-a-kind hybrid prized by the Almighty.

And to the future CEOs in my doctoral seminar at
Capella University—what a gutsy, creative, and protean
bunch of hybrids they were!

CONTENTS

THE REARRANGER

THE ANTICIPATOR

THE INTEGRATOR

THE INNOVATOR

Introduction

L EADERSHIP AUDIENCES ARE SPECIAL and different in at least three ways. First, they are demanding. Whether composed of eager doctoral candidates or impatient upper-level managers, they always claim to know more than you do—or always want more than you have to offer—and inevitably accuse experts of major sins of omission. How could you have left out this or that critical leadership trait or, worse, how could you have given such short shift to or ignored completely the latest book or leadership guru?

Second, leadership experts are perceived as biased and favor one kind of leadership over all the others. The rationale for such preferences is prescriptive—that is precisely the kind of visionary we urgently need now if we are to be guided through current uncertainty. Even when the preference is not specific but generic, such as primal or intellectual leadership, such partiality still is unfortunately limiting.

But their worst crime is that they have not facilitated choice. That is, in our desire to be objective, expert, and complex, we have concluded by leaving everything up in the air, and, like all leadership experts, we have even relished being inconclusive so that cynically and selfishly we can return to the podium and go on teaching and lecturing on leadership forever and enjoying again and again—all protests notwithstanding—the martyrdom of being misunderstood.

The last objection is perhaps the most serious because it obscures or trivializes the basic motivation and focus of an audience of aspiring leaders. To be sure, the experts defend such deflection by noting that it applies not solely to the purveyors of leadership, but also to the subject itself. Routinely treated as the holy of holies, leadership is often so exalted that at times it rivals a religious quest. It is reserved for the exceptional and inspirational few who are routinely hailed and haloed as if they emerged from scripture. And the ritual is reenacted each year in the publication of some two thousand books and articles consumed by those seeking the magic bullet or formula to make it to the top. The net result is a kind of complicity between teachers and learners, between those who want to preserve the mystery and those who are eager to wrap themselves in its mystical mantle—between the desire to permanently keep it open-ended and the need for some sort of reasonable closure.

Over the years I typically have favored the first group of leadership pontificators and sermonizers. But of late I have found myself increasingly and more sympathetically drawn to the second group of aspiring practitioners and their desire for explicit guidance. Why? It struck me—we make so much ado about the executive decision-making process that we fail to acknowledge that the most important leadership decision of all is choosing what kind of leader to be. In fact, it is nothing less than who you are—your leadership bedrock. Nothing else comes close to setting you apart and driving everything you do. It also later becomes your brand—how you are known in the industry; how the executive recruiters classify you in their files; and finally what kind of followers want to hitch their wagon to your star.

Sympathy for the plight of such aspiring and embryonic leaders requires answers to their compelling questions. What do they want to know? Middle-level managers want to know what the next steps are in their upward climb. Upper-level heads of divisions or vice presidents want to know what kind of leader they have to be to get them to and over the top. And finally, even chief executive officers (CEOs) already there want to know what it will take to keep them there.

In other words, all are poised at different stages to make career-breaking choices. But three obstacles stand in the way. The first is choice—spelling out and profiling the basic leadership options, displaying their full range and depth, their upsides and downsides, their history and their future. The second is positioning such options in a context—a continuum of adaptability to facilitate leadership development and evolution. That requires rejecting the notion that, unlike all other professionals, leaders do not grow, and that a choice once made precludes making others. The third is understanding and acknowledging that the leadership developmental process of growing out of one's skin, as it were, follows a seldom-defined pattern of cumulative development in which past roles are not so much discarded as adjusted to meet new challenges.

The net result is thus not a singular but a multiple profile, not one component or a series but a composite, not one direction but a circular process—in short, a new norm, the hybrid leader. Addressing and removing such obstacles, prospective leaders, as well as the readers of leadership books, are offered the following conclusions:

1. Leadership choices are known and available, their range is current and their depth demonstrable, and the direction of their vision and mission definable. In short, choice is thus fully facilitated.
2. Selection is not a one-shot grab at the golden ring. Leaders have many options available all along the way to evolve and develop new identities. In short, nimble and agile leaders and their companies enjoy the proverbial nine lives.
3. Paradoxically, the development dynamic for leaders is both unique and individually designed. It is meant to image a new kind of growth pattern—multidirectional and more inclusive, unfinished, time evolving, and change driven. In short, it is an ongoing continuum.

To turn to the first major obstacle: the general absence of a list of choices. That is not the case here. Leadership does not become impoverished, robbed of its secrets, or lose its integrity by explicitly identifying its range. The claim here is that there are essentially five basic options, laid out here as the classic and recurrent choices that over the years leaders have chosen separately or in combined fashion as their unique blend of talent and task. They are as follows:

The Changer
The Rearranger

The Integrator
The Innovator
The Anticipator

These five choices are what this book is about. This book considers what they are, what they do, how they are chosen, by whom, when, and why they are chosen, whether there is a preference of one over another, whether they are ever combined, and what their characteristic behaviors and misbehaviors are. Answers to these and other questions follow, but the first chapter, as all beginnings do, has to complicate both the inquiry and the journey.

Prologue: Mapping the Journey

WRITING A BOOK IS NOT THE SAME as compiling it. Writing is more driven, urgent, and reflective. It is directed at your field and the colleagues who inhabit and define it. Often, it may single out those with whom you disagree. That is why each book rightly is called an argument—an assertive thesis not necessarily advanced in a mean or contentious way but nevertheless focused and designed to rival and sometimes replace the arguments of others.

But putting it all together is a different matter. That is essentially under the influence of readers. Not subject to contention or manipulation, they occupy the center and drive book design. Although certainly not slighted in the writing, they nevertheless have not received the kind of formative, comprehensive, and specific attention they deserve. The reader is now in the driver's seat, but not in any general or generic way. In particular, there are three special and differentiated reader types.

First and above all, there are all the aspirants—all those who are hot to trot and eager to lead. They rightly insist on knowing what it will take to get there, whether they have the right stuff and grit to go all the way, what the next steps are, and how to be set apart and recognized for their executive potential. Even those who already are on top want to know how to stay there and what they have to contend with in the new crop of those on the rise. If it were up to them, the book would be designed as a manual.

Next are all the internal leader-related professionals and departments linked to executive decisions and initiatives. They run the range of the entire organization. Indeed, it can be argued that each CEO operates within a preferred constellation of business disciplines, from among, for example, the financial, information technology (IT), human resources (HR), and strategic planning teams, and that what kind of leader he is can be rapidly defined by his structural allies. In any case, they worry about being included or excluded from the magic circle of executive orbit. They thus seek positioning. They also want to know who is in and who is out, what new face they have to assume to be among the chosen, and what strategies they have to achieve status. They would prefer the book be a board game in the form of an organizational chart in which hopefully they regularly cross "Go," collect $200, and emerge as winners.

Finally, there are a number of important external players not without influence who traffic in cutting-edge developments as their life blood and competitive advantage. These are all the management consultants, executive coaches, executive headhunters, editors of leadership magazines, publishers of leadership books, heads of expensive executive global development leadership programs, designers of leadership testing and assessment profiles, and so forth. They are all interested parties. And although they appear objective, they are lobbyists. If they had their way, the book would be a handbook of applications and preferred users with a suggested range of billables.

What to do? Clearly, book design cannot ignore those who read and buy books. So authors have to satisfy all three groups but—and this is the tricky part—in ways that preserve their passion on the one hand and the book's integrity on the other.

How to do that? First, by acknowledging and giving weight to the existence and value of each urgent point of view; second, by persuading them that their passionate self-interest is differently but happily served by the book's argument; and third, by assuring them that their partial and limited advocacy is not only honored but also given greater extent and applications by the wider parameters of the book's range. In other words, in the final analysis, each book in its argument and compilation constitutes a vision of the field that includes all its readers. Thus, the book is divided into three parts.

The first part facilitates leadership choice for all aspirants. It converges four arguments: that there are five basic and classic leadership options; that although distinct they overlap to the point where they can attain a blended or hybrid quality; that leaders over time can evolve into, develop, and become such amalgams; and finally that there are no time or situational limits on when and how that can happen because leaders are ultimately unfinished. The book then is a kind of manual in that it sets out the fundamental taxonomy of leadership types. But it is also *not* a manual because choice, on the one hand, is ultimately too obsessive and mysterious to be mechanical or predictable and, on the other hand, it is without end.

The second group of leadership-dependent readers is honored in a special way. Although the five leadership types display a clarity and precision over time, they have to take on, survive, emerge, and manage their identity through an incredible diversity of situations and contexts. Indeed, many of those departments and professionals have contributed to and even created the organizational changes over time that CEOs have inherited and have finally to make their own. So it seemed fitting and appropriate to follow the basic types with a comprehensive review of many of the key organizational challenges and conditions that leaders of all types have had to face and overcome and that have raised the need for leaders to blend types and to become hybrids in the first place. In other words, the middle portion of the book is a record of the gauntlet of organizational change that all twenty-first-century executives have to confront, manage, and lead their way through as conditions and definitions of their leadership. But instead of being an aggressive game of whose ox is gored, the compilation and analysis of all those essential variables and situations that shape the style and brand of all five leadership types is neutral, giving all their due. At the same time, it offers an impressive catalog of all the changes many have independently wrought to alter the leadership landscape.

Finally, the last group has been honored by returning to the beginning and profiling separately each of the five major types. But this time typology is integrated with the variables of organizational contexts and situations so that hopefully what emerges is a three-dimensional version of form and content, person and function, vision and mission. In some happy cases, such profiles have even generated new forms of executive interview questions.

But by reaching back to where we started, we are again providing those who aspire not only the basic leadership models, but also the tough, stirring, and heady journey of the climb to the top, reserved ultimately for the unfinished and unclassifiable.

COMPLICATING AND CHALLENGING CHOICE

I

Choice Criteria: Decisive and Persuasive 1

LEADERSHIP CHOICE SUMS UP THE CHOOSER. It is his primary color, his signature, his fingerprint. But neither the process nor the outcome is easy or mechanical. It is not one size fits all. You can be conservative or outrageous, boring or totally compulsive. The parameters of leadership choices are elastic and forgiving; there is always room for shading, styling, and even idiosyncrasies.

But no one gets there instantly or directly or without pain, deflection, and false starts. Dead ends are norms. The process is encumbered from the outset with a devilish mix of complications and challenges, which only afterward may turn out to be benevolent and indispensable. Like knights of old, aspiring novices have to undergo a series of rituals of preparation. In more modern terms, they often take the form of wise warnings of what not to do or what to avoid doing. Frequently ignored, the impact is often harsh but not fatal. Later, they are often affirmed and become part of the extensive and insightful literature of wise warnings offered now to others. Indeed, the next few chapters present a sample of such foolproof forearming and forewarning examples associated with leadership choice and definition.

But all agree on one principle: there is no avoiding or postponing choice. Choice is a conscious decision. It needs to be anticipated and contemplated way before circumstances and choices are thrust upon you. What you choose should not be determined by others or from without. Finally, you should not lose the opportunity to honor the special career path that is a unique match for your talent.

You also have to be involved in shaping your shadow—your brand. It is what persuades those around you to be your followers; it leads them to embrace your driving difference. That, in turn, perpetuates, advertises, and further sets you and your brand of leadership apart. Although all leaders are obsessive in what they choose to do, not all compulsions are alike. So there is a need for leaders to distinguish themselves—to appear as one of a kind. Fortunately, there is a way to make the unique generic. The worst kind of leader is vanilla—interchangeable, always sounding like all the other executives, and surrounded by look-alike associates all wearing the same jackets and ties. But the initial choice of talent involves a second choice: branding what you have chosen so that it now identifies your niche, stakes out your singular style, and suggests all the other talents that are now hidden but available later.

Why is brand so important? Because it is not enough to take the lead; it has to be self-evident and persuasive, reassuring, attention-grabbing, smart and understated, and possess a curve of energy. No matter how outrageous it may sometimes be, leadership has to resonate with and acquire an immediately sympathetic audience. Above all, it has to be always open, inviting, and sharing, as leadership is the ultimate form of communication. The leader is the supreme communicator, and his recurrent message is the nature of his leadership.

Leaders have to be both decisive and persuasive. Brand defines not only what you have decided to do but signals why and how. It automatically scans the range of descriptors and selects only those that set your leadership apart. It is the shorthand version of executive command. Brand is unmistakable, tyrannical, and nontransferable. It confirms again and again your characteristic leadership decisions, behaviors, and even style. It is your trademark.

Brand is also tenacious. If, along the way, circumstances change to the point where you are no longer a fit with the kind of leadership your company wants and what your talent provides, so powerful and determining is brand that, rather than choosing to change, the CEO will choose to leave—or hopefully be offered another command that taps his brand and what it uniquely has to offer.

But leadership and brand selection do not occur in a vacuum; it is an evolving process that determines the nature of that executive stamp. Like the choice of what kind of leader you seek to be, brand selection is not free of determiners. Brand building rests on a number of prior choices or outcomes—specifically, the convergence of three: the personal, the circumstantial, and the preferential.

The first is who we are and how we have come to be that way—the composite make-up of our native talents and drives, how the psychology and sociology of family and society have prepared and programmed us to be, and whether we were born leaders or acquired leaders or a mix of both. The second input is comprised of the external challenges and problems being faced by the culture of the organization we join or head up. The embrace in fact is inevitably historical—where we are at and where business and country are at in time. Thus, in a sense, all leadership is dated—the latest but not the final version of a historical continuum. Finally, after taking into account and allowing for the impact of the first two contributing factors, we run into the problem mentioned at the outset; choice is not facilitated.

Leadership options are typically not spelled out. To be sure the leadership literature displays, classifies, and analyzes leadership patterns as an objective exercise, but choice is not invited. Surprisingly, it is often absent even in company leadership development programs where one would expect explicit guidance and where academic paralysis seldom operates. Of course, the curricula of most executive leadership MBA or PhD programs routinely stop short of accommodating the key question of deciding what kind of leader to be.

Even later when prestigious institutes offer seasoned and experienced CEOs short seminars, they are always about getting smarter at what they are already doing rather than offering what is the new need—how, why, and when to trade in old spots and stripes and become another kind of leader. Why, then, is leadership choice postponed, avoided, deflected, or even ignored—treated as a taboo or private subject between you and your therapist or mentor?

In many ways it is understandable. No one wants to be held responsible for influencing the choice of a major professional direction, let alone one so critical as a leadership role. Mentors and coaches do not want to be around to pick up the pieces when and if their advice or guidance turns out to be faulty. But still it comes down to making a choice.

The five options laid out here stake out the basic choices that over the years have guided others and are designed to encourage informed choices. They are shown below:

The Changer (Transformational)
The Rearranger (Transactional)
The Integrator (Convergent)
The Innovator (Entrepreneur)
The Anticipator (Futuristic)

Before premature objections of oversimplification cloud the issue, let me quickly complicate the claim. My argument is that the five choices above are archetypal and summative. They identify the basic historical choices in their most essential forms over time. Do the categories overlap? Of course. In fact, they are meant to. And if not chosen initially, are they never again available? On the contrary, nothing is ever discarded. All that is not chosen can later be recycled—reconfigured—and subsumed to be aligned with and supportive of the initial basic leadership choice. Thus every leader who is primarily transformational in nature also possesses the potential of all the other remaining talents. He has the capacity to alter organizational design, integrate and optimize units and disciplines, bring innovation to the forefront, and of course be futuristic. The difference is that in the process each of the remaining leadership factors are enlisted and defined by the dominant one to the point where, individually and collectively, they acquire a unique hierarchy of identity.

The proportions and territoriality of each is determined and negotiated from the top. They are all variables called on to step up and minister to changing organizational circumstances and leaderships. In this sense leaders lead from within as well as without; their reserves are marshaled internally to match the composition of the external challenge. They are also by definition unfinished. They are all ultimately hybrids who enrich and extend their identity by linking, learning, and leveraging.

However, lists are a necessary evil—sometimes more evil than necessary. They provide clarity, but in the process they have a way of disguising or obscuring dynamic interplay. They also favor hierarchy and imply that what appears first is preferred. That is why I prefer displaying the range of choices in the arrangement of a pentagram and why leadership needs to be both clear and complicated—explicit to facilitate choice, and multiple to serve as the building block of brand. The initial choice prepares for the follow-up threshold of subsequent choices.

The net result is a leadership profile that is multiply layered and faceted and that in turn feeds upon itself and its historical partners to generate a whole and a brand equal to the task of being a comprehensive leader for all seasons. But the basic argument remains: The above leadership options are classic, recurrent, and defining, and they remain so even in their reinforcing roles. They never disappear or lose their integrity. Like reserves, they stand ready to be called into the game plan by the quarterback calling the plays. In this sense leadership is always a team-like activity.

But although we welcome such richness, it is critical that we keep our eye on the ball and stake out for aspiring managers the major leadership directions that support and facilitate their sorting out process. They serve as scaffolding to frame the inquiry of what kind of leader they should be. Each one is profiled as a three-dimensional character in a play in which they are the star and always play the leading role. But equally as important, the commitment to leadership choice and branding in turn is anchored in a comprehensive set of assumptions about leadership in general, which are reflected in the following ten central themes of this book:

1. Leadership choices are known and knowable.
2. They are not singular but multiple.
3. But the range is limited to a relative few, which support a robust taxonomy.
4. Leadership houses not just one basic choice but many. There is always a dominant one, which often is frozen into exclusivity by talent or success. But all the other options are always there to be called on.

5. Leadership roles and choices are archetypal and classic. The test of all current leaders is to combine the old and new, the recurrent and familiar, the obvious and radical, and the cyclical and unique.

6. Leadership is both inherently driven and externally shaped—compulsive and chosen. Leaders are born, made, unmade, and remade. Leaders are never finished.

7. Leadership branding sets the executive apart—doubly—by how he leads and how he communicates leadership.

8. All leaders are ultimately one of a kind—by choice, by brand, by internal design, and finally by the unique organizational circumstances and history of what they lead.

9. Leadership is also differentiated by the kind of followers it attracts. The range includes disciples, yes men, "yes but" types, coequals, colleagues, associates, and so forth. Followers thus make choices as well—not only about what kind of leader they emulate and in turn may want to be but also what kind of follower they want to be and what they need to learn.

10. Leadership produces a special kind of leadership savvy and smarts. Developed over time, it is a unique way of thinking and knowing, of root-cause problem solving, framing elusive and contradictory issues, and converging talent and circumstance.

The burden of this book-long exploration, then, is to describe and analyze these choices to help you decide what kind of leader and direction you need to pursue to get you uniquely to the top; if you are already or nearly there, contemplate and bring to the surface other leadership directions and create a new match of talent and circumstances; for both groups, create new leadership hybrid brands that are uniquely yours and yet born both of this time and of the future of our age—and to do so with executive distinction; and in the process also value directional choice.

Directional Leadership: All the Points of the Compass 2

IF WE WERE TO HEARKEN TO THE FINDINGS of cognitive psychologists who are closer and closer to cracking the cerebral code, discussion of decision-making should be preceded by examining how we think our way through the complicated process of choosing in the first place. We also would be urged to note that thinking enjoys a special, intimate, and knowing relationship with what it contemplates, chooses, and endorses.

In other words, Robert Frost's selection of the road less traveled is not accidental or undriven. Frost is a loner, finding distinction and even creativity by being numbered among the few. He thinks of himself and his craft as singular and solitary—off to the side—and the periphery as the best way to the center. In other words, without presuming a one-to-one correlation between a poet's life and work, it is safer and more revealing to find a linkage between his thinking and his choosing.

Similarly, J. P. Donleavy thinks about making his way through the world by his wits and his agility. "Jack be nimble, Jack be quick" and "now you see me, now you don't" sum up not only how he survives but also how he sees reality—as something out to get you, as a daily test of the talent of direction-changing and eluding nets. Given such thinking the choice of being clever and an escape artist makes a great deal of sense.

Leaders are no different. The selection of direction is influenced by their thinking about that direction. Indeed, some leaders are known to be so predisposed to certain options that it becomes their brand—even to the point where they are hired because of their expertise in changing unhappy directions for ones with more promise. When Howard Gardner sought to apply cognitive psychology to the task of classifying choices, he did so in terms of minds—in his case, five future minds.

In effect, Gardner developed cognitively centered choices, most of which surprisingly resemble the leadership choices advocated here. In short, one of the key steps in evolving the definition of each direction will be to seek to identify and examine the thinking and expectations that that choice appears to generate and attract.

Leadership Directions
Each leadership choice embodies a preferred direction, as follows:

Transformational—Vertical
Transactional—Horizontal
Integrator—Lateral
Innovative—Leapfrog
Anticipator—Circular

To demonstrate how directional choice can define and even determine leadership behavior and brand, let us use the transformational as an example (later all the others will be similarly examined). If ever history could claim one direction over all others, it would be this one. Pyramidal and ascending, it embodies hierarchy and order. It enshrines empires, religions, and organizational charts. It is the epitome of bureaucracy as well, always busy putting one layer above another, one ruler or supervisor over rank and file, and in the process establishing orderly succession up the ladder.

An entrepreneur would be a misfit in this vertical world; if he survived, he would be forced to behave like Donleavy. But the chain of command is absolute and unforgiving, or, as Nietzsche wisely warned, "I skip steps and no step will ever forgive you for skipping it." Loved and even worshipped by the military, the vertical became the favored way to manage a new wilderness or a conquered people. Indeed, Rome (like all empire builders) exported and replicated its top-down structure all over the world. In fact, its ability to take hold in such varied climes and cultures was touted as proof of both the superiority of the conqueror and the infallibility of the management system.

And obviously it worked for decades and even centuries, although stretching too far out often jeopardized control and invoked the law of diminishing returns. Hitler and Stalin, linking a universal ideology with worldwide domination, tried to achieve a secular version of religious evangelism in the last century but failed, leaving the pope as the supreme ruler of the vertical.

This way of regulating up and down also became the favored form of capitalism for three basic goals: to manage size, to exercise control, and to extract profitability. Once manufacturing and business in the nineteenth century discovered mass production and the correlation of units and man hours, modern management was born. Followed soon thereafter by marketing, scientific management came to the fore by linking efficiency to earnings and discovering through experimentation at Bethlehem Steel how many shovels per minute yielded the most profits. Later, when greater gains were sought, it was employed to determine how to increase the size of the shovel.

Is the pyramid obsolete today? Far from it. In fact, one of the distinctive features of the global economy is the coexistence of virtually every direction and every phase of the economic evolution of capitalism somewhere in the planet. In addition, some multinationals are still exporting and replicating their pyramids abroad, now tied together and managed electronically.

To be sure, with outsourcing of functions and distribution of supply centers, the monolith has been tamed and reduced in size and extent. In addition, the sources of profits have been enhanced by shifting from more to less expensive workers and suppliers. And finally, management by metrics and software has replaced the last of the third rationale for capitalistic management of the vertical.

Although the vertical persists in less familiar, total, and dominant forms in the United States and abroad, it remains as the favored direction of those who still value command and control. Like generals, such leaders are drawn to the combat of competition and to the rallying call of being supreme in the field and industry. In this connection it may not be so surprising then that so many ex-generals are called upon to lead governments and corporations. The prospect of molding and marshaling a motley group of uneven workers and an assortment of different parts into one unified and dedicated force still holds enormous appeal for those leaders who believe they have the talent and the stomach for just that kind of ennobling and heroic effort.

Their thinking is Darwinian and is predicated on Arnold Toynbee's famous exhortation: "The greater the challenge the greater the response." Vertical leaders believe professionals and companies need such challenges to get the juices flowing and to realize their performance potential—of what they can be and do. They also believe they uniquely have the capacity to develop a vision to achieve such distinction and the inspiration to motivate what it takes to get there.

The vertical is thus inevitably the favored choice of the transformational leader who in fact needs size and reluctance to demonstrate his transformation power and whose charisma is enough to carry the day. Although (strangely perhaps) they also would understand and appreciate the less-traveled road of Frost and occasional clever pulling-the-rabbit-out-of-the-hat of Donleavy, they nevertheless would expect such types to be joiners not loners and to become part of a new whole on the move.

But lest one conclude that the vertical is solely the monopoly of transformational leaders and inevitably accompanied by bravado and rallying slogans, there are some quieter and more analytical signs that it is being chosen as a leadership pathway for reasons at variance from its more rigid and hierarchical history. The overall direction remains vertical but now moves not up but down, courts not the heights but the depths. The transactional replaces the transformational, the situational for the visionary, as transformation and vision stop being the sole objects of leadership and are replaced by or forced to share the stage with the less glamorous but persuasive nature of process. Charisma is now tamed and paired with analysis. In other words, the image of the commanding leader does not disappear, but he becomes less official and more dispensable—not so much a star on the stage as a guide on the side. He advocates rather than commands.

We need to pause here to appreciate the way leadership directions work and evolve. They are all absolutes—primordial and archetypal, permanently built into existence and history. They have been around and been the favored choices and objects of veneration and even worship since leading itself was an option. But there are minimally three variables, in ascending order of difficulty.

The first is cultural. The choice of direction is influenced by the zeitgeist—the prevailing values of the times and those that lead. Conversely, what is overwhelmingly chosen tells us much about the society's values and preferences, especially if the process of selection was contested. Indeed, often support of one direction is inspired by the fear of a less appealing one coming in and taking over. Thus, all directions may be dressed up in different historical clothes but their essentials remain solid, intact, and recognizable.

The second variable is more challenging largely because it has the potential to become an alternative, to break off and set up its own independent and often competing camp. Typically that does not happen because all the fundamental directions are flexible and ac- commodating. The basic directions would not have survived as long as they have if they were not open to accept variations on a theme. But even when open collision shatters coexistence, when the normal tension is replaced by open opposition, and the split is official, overt, and out in the open, the contest remains recognizable. The gladia- tors embody the essential directions. Although not always easily perceived, what they champion gradually defines their allegiance.

The final one is often the most challenging. All leadership direc- tions have applications—ways of putting their driving principles into practice. But some may appear to be self-spawned, self-contained, unlinked to any mother ship. Such radical standalones betray a ge- netic source. Their methodologies illustrate larger principles and origins—and, when finally linked and reunited to their source, gain greater currency and classic value.

The Transformational Culture of Next!

We still tend to pay attention to leaders who are different—who set themselves apart by what they do, what they say, and often by how they think. We particularly value those who are not bland or inhabit the shadows. We prefer the visible and vigorous who are knowl- edgeable about their business and industry, speak their minds, explain their decisions, and do not play it safe or indulge in predictable platitudes but openly are champions. At their best they combine savvy and smarts, but they do not claim to be geniuses or parade their high IQ. Besides, as Fred Smith, CEO of FedEx, has wisely reminded us, the outstanding violinist or top hitter probably would not make the best conductor or coach. In other words, the determining factor is not performance but leading performance.

That, again and again, is their distinction. They love to be out front and in charge, they cherish the affirmation of followers, and they work hard and long. When asked for advice they typically claim that leading is learnable. It is a craft, a skill, a style, and it is addictive. But preeminently it is always actionable. It is in the doing, especially in doing things differently and creatively. That trait when added to two others forms the leadership trinity: the ability to read the times, to remain unfinished, and to do things differently.

We are accustomed to regard the forces around us as not of our own making—as a given of history. Our task is somehow to make sense of what we have inherited, and play the hand dealt to us. But that is not what vertical leaders do. They read the times. They do not accept the given. They do not regard anything as immutable or fixed in stone. They test, they probe, and they turn things on their head. And they do so by being doers. They don't understand any other way. To them reality is a contest to see who comes out on top, which vision prevails, and which company survives, grows, and outlasts the others. They view their role of leader as neither a time server nor a passive observer of the passing scene. Instead, the leader is a constant combatant who never ignores challenges or leaves them intact or unmet, and who aggressively, confidently, and quietly goes about the business of being smarter and more imaginative than the competition. And, if in the process the leader is able to persuade others not only to follow his lead but also to add their unique gifts to the repertoire of doing things differently, then he is justified in being in charge and earning the big bucks.

It is at this point where the charisma of "Follow me" and the vision of a brave new world may be not enough. Savvy has to find an ally in smarts. The characteristic response of those who wish to lead change is initially and always more mundane and down to earth.

Instead of the bold leap forward, they ask again and again "Next!"—as in "Okay, but what's the next step?" or "What is the next issue?" or "Where do we go from here?" or "What's Plan B?" or "How far out and fast do we have to go just to catch up let alone get ahead?" Next! gradually becomes a new constant. There is never a lull; nothing is ever finally over or done with. Indeed, sometimes the function of a solution is to expose a bigger problem—to get to the next Next!

Such leaders are restless—always coming and going, alternately playing catch up and thinking ahead. They seem always to be in a hurry, impatient about the way things and we are—in a condition of flux, locked in a permanent state of transition. If in the process we are discomforted, it stems partly from uncertainty, but mostly from not making peace and accepting that this crazy pace at which we have to live and work may be a new norm—the way reality really is.

And yet, although that is exactly the way we have been living and working for a decade at least, we typically resist accepting all the adjustments we have made as final. We step back and refuse to embrace what, in effect, is a new divide. To be sure, we have handled and come to terms with managing change, but not this—not being broken off from history, to face a twenty-first century of Next! That is totally different and discontinuous. Indeed, if it were not for leaders who find this brave new world bracing and manageable, we might despair or yearn for the nostalgia of the good old days.

But the ultimate claim is that the way things are is the way our leaders are. The restless and probing way they lead has put a mark on the way all of us do things and upon the acceptance of process as never ending. They are the preeminent leaders of transition, which replaces transformation as the new norm and operating definition of reality. As a result there is little stillness and finality to our lives and work anymore because we are always living and working ahead of ourselves and of our time. While we were not looking, the future slid into the present. We thus have become more aware of the hidden and multiple consequences of our actions and of living continuing learning lives. Above all we welcome and follow leaders who are no longer content with fast fixes or passing of halves as wholes. And nowhere is this better exemplified than the adoption and adaptation of the "Next!" approach of rallying leaders to virtually all problem-solving and business operations. Indeed, it has taken hold to such an extent that it has been the major force for the creation of the culture of Next!

The ideology of the culture of Next! rests on three don'ts:

1. Don't ever stop too soon or short of the next Next!
2. Don't settle for less than 100 percent or 360 degrees or win-win.
3. Don't just ask about know-how but also about know-why, until you get to the root cause.

What follows is a familiar example of Next! in action.

When something goes wrong on the production line or an important game or a big deal is lost, what happens? Typically, the blame, shame, and gotcha game surfaces complete with finger pointing. After allowing venting time, the manger-leader begins the post-mortem process by invoking and applying the above three rules of Next! to the problem. The key is to get beyond symptoms to causes, finally to root causes. Here is how Next! handles the Q&A of fault-finding:

Q. "OK, why did the machine fail?"

A. "It was not properly maintained according to specs."

This where the questions usually stop. Why? Because most inquiries are perceived as fault-finding expeditions and once the villain is exposed one need not go further. It makes no difference that the answer is partial or premature. Once the butler is chosen as the usual suspect, the murder mystery is over.

But manager-leaders who subscribe to Next! and value Kaizen, the Japanese system of asking "Why?" at least five times, press on and on until they hit pay dirt—the root cause of the problem. Because then and only then do correctives make sense and take on the quality of a 360-degree solution. But now back to the Next! process.

Q. "Why was it not maintained?"

A. "The maintenance schedule was reduced."

Q. "Why was it reduced?"

A. "To eliminate one maintainer and save money."

Q. "Who made that decision?"

A. "Finance officer and HR."

Q. "Was the plant manager consulted?"

A. "No, but he became aware of it when he reviewed the monthly roster."

Q. "And what did he do then?"

A. "Nothing. It was a done deed."

Okay, let us stop now and tally up all that we have learned so far. But in the process of identifying all that is problematic here, let us also go into solution mode so that such breakdowns either won't happen or are immediately more manageable. Here are the essentials:

- We have a maintenance schedule, but we don't have a preventative maintenance policy.
- Among other things, that policy would establish chain of command and consulting.
- We have specs from the manufacturer, but we have not spelled out in detail what can break down and what it would cost. Thus, we have not made a case in financial terms of the impact of equipment breakdown—of what can happen, the worst-case scenario—if we take shortcuts.
- That cost-impact study has to be compiled and delivered by the plant manager to the finance officer and HR.
- Above all, we have failed to build in risk factors—including breakdowns—into all scheduling and planning and create contingencies.
- Hopefully what we have learned is that when a machine fails, more than that has failed.
- And that, if fault is to be found, it is collective.

But for Next! to become company-wide and not just preached at cheerleading orientations and at PR sessions, CEOs also need to change the boss mentality that values obedience over initiative and that typically exclaims, "We are not paying you to think," for that is exactly what we want this new overqualified workforce to do and what they are uniquely qualified to do. Finally, the sage warning of Robert Frost should be applied to the entire HR process: "Before I built a wall I'd ask to know/What I was walling in or walling out." Good fences may make for good neighbors but they don't make for savvy employees who think outside and beyond the boundaries— and practice the culture of Next!

In summary, then, there is a culture of Next! in all sectors, in all industries, and at all levels. But wherever and whenever you find it working its magic, there you will find not only leadership at work but also the leverage of learning—the fusion of savvy and smarts. Above all, you will always begin to sense an emerging future, for that is always the ultimate next Next!—a new yield from the depths of the vertical and horizontal, the emerging definition of the leader as process, as transition.

The Five-Star Leadership Taxonomy **3**

THE AIM HERE IS TO PROFILE THE range of basic leadership choices and to do so with sufficient depth so that they appear tangible, real, and different. Whatever cross-overs and overlapping may occur can be taken up and made part of individual profiles. Four categories are used throughout to classify the five basic leadership types. They appear in both the summary and elaborated versions. These favored and recurrent short descriptors have been compiled over time from doctoral students in leadership development programs.

Elaborated Version
Profile of the Changer
ROLE

    The Climber

    The Driver

Table 3.1. Leadership Types Summary

Role	Focus	Modes	Direction	Outcomes
1. The Changer	Transformation	Action/Aspiration	Vertical	New Vision
2. The Rearranger	Transactional	Interface/Teaming	Horizontal	New Structures
3. The Integrator	Holistic	360 Networking	Zig-Zag Clusters	New Composites
4. The Anticipator	Leapfrogging	Transitioning	Out Front/Ahead	New Cyborgs
5. The Innovator	Inventive	Convergence	Circular	New Amalgams

The Lone Ranger
Type-A Personality
Action-Oriented
Gut Instinct
Workaholic
One-Man Show
Takes over Everything
All Grist for the Mill of Change
Genius Leadership
Great Man
Big Idea
Busy
Indispensable
The Savior

FOCUS

Review and Eliminate
Alter to Align
Shape Up or Resign
Our Way or the Highway
Get with the Program
Energy and Enthusiasm
Leave Nothing Intact
Driven toward Excellence

MODES

Rallying
Cheerleading
Inspirational Retreats
Bonuses for Winners
A Star System
Loyalty
CEO Knows Best
Endless Improvement
Balanced Score Card

DIRECTION

Upward
No End in Sight

Sky Is the Limit
Highest ROI
Industry Leader
Hierarchical
Pyramidal
Chain of Command

OUTCOMES
New Stirring Vision of Company
Branded Excellence
Measuring Transformation
Before and After
Celebration of Growth/Change
Next Ten-Year Plan
"Ain't Seen Nothing Yet!"

Profile of the Rearranger

ROLE
Reorganizer of Everything
Consolidator
Interfacer
Networker
Negotiator
Restructurer
Outsourcer
RIF
Relater
Researcher
Servant Leader

FOCUS
Increased Productivity
Greater Profitability
Cost/Time Savings
Continuous Improvement
Transparency
Accountability

State of the Art
Best Practices
Teaming Culture

MODES
More with Less
Kaizen—Root Cause
Conflict Resolution
Internal Customers
Involving Customers in Improvements

DIRECTION
Horizontal
Across the Board
Divisional Interfacing
Customer Interfacing

OUTCOMES
New Teaming Structure
Higher ROI and Profitability
More Efficient Networking

Profile of the Integrator

ROLE
Uniter
Intersecter
Converger
Asking Why
Includer
Synergist
Knowledge Pusher
Frontier Challenger

FOCUS
More
Bigger
More Inclusive

Holistics
360-Degree
Virtual Teaming
Singularity

MODES
Lateral Thinking
Cross-Thinking
Intersectional Knowledge
Human-Machine Identity

DIRECTION
Left and Right
Up and Down
Diagonal and Across
Circular

OUTCOMES
New Organizational Composites
New Human Amalgams
New Hybrids

Profile of the Anticipator

ROLE
Leapfrogger
What If?
Trender
Science Fictionist
Living Ahead
End Gamer
Projector
Prophet
Entrepreneur

FOCUS
What's Ahead
What's Next

Disruptive
Gaps
New Frontiers
Outer Space
Under Seas
Apocalypse
Cornucopia
Succession Planning

MODES
Forecasts
Trends
Markets
Scenarios
Survival Games
Transition Training
End Games

DIRECTIONS
Beginnings and Ends
History of the Far Out and Ways
Future of the Past
Up in Space
Down in Water
Ahead to Year 3000

OUTCOMES
New States of Being
New Worlds
New Orders
New Solutions
New Succession Plans

Profile of the Innovator
ROLE
Leverager
Intersector

Out of Boxer
What About
Assumptions Challenger
Science Fictionist
Synergist
Non-Incrementalist

FOCUS
Time Space
Utopia/Dystopia
Ask Problem to Solve Itself
Child Think
Play

MODES
Brainstorm
Jack Be Nimble
Lateral Thinking
360-Degree
Ultimate Solutions
Endgames

DIRECTIONS
Backward
Way Ahead
Around the Corner
Inside Out
Upside Down

OUTCOMES
New Products
New Services
New Businesses
New Careers

But critical though the above are, they are still the raw materials of the next phase of branding.

The Impacts of Size and Teams on Leadership

4

I N THE PAST, HARDLY ANYONE QUESTIONED that bigger was better. It was proof of growth, market share, and stability. After all, there was the comfort of being too big to fail. These giants were so secure and generous that, like universities, they could grant managers the largesse of tenure. But when things changed radically and competition took hold of the jugular, such excesses were difficult to correct largely because such practices were no longer the only problem. The issue had become not what the companies were but what they were not. They were not quick, agile, and swift. They were obedient, predictable, and cocksure.

Scale and structure became mirror images. Size compels distance, from the top and from what was on the right or left. Everything was boxed and boxed-in. Accountability to stockholders was high but inventiveness was low. Coasting became the norm. People were busy but energy was always contained. Under-performing became routine. Then, because desperation, not enlightenment, is often the mother of invention, what was considered immutable—scale and structure—became variable, and experimentation with small-scale structures began to take place.

Big corporations created smaller businesses within the larger business. Profit centers consisting of one hundred to two hundred employees were cobbled together. In manufacturing, the singularity of the production line gave way to the manufacturing cell. In many companies, teaming and cross-training became a new way of doing business. Other organizations opted for distributed leadership based on contribution rather than title. Other groups created futures teams of one hundred or so professionals within an organization charged with engaging the territory ahead. And so on.

Scale and structure combined to create miniatures of the whole, little worlds made close. When these new forms prospered it was because they were given their own way and budget. They were not forced to reflect or obey the culture of their offspring. But when the umbilical cord was tenaciously maintained, so that when they were asked to run their legs in effect were tied, they faltered and failed.

If one examines the characteristics and qualities of the most successful experimental smaller versions of their parental forms and their respective impacts on leadership, at least five essential factors emerge.

Communication

Small groups or structures up the ante on communications. In fact, that is what holds the group together. They constantly talk things out. They discover ignorance or arrogance that way, and search for the cause of either or both. The job, including its problems and obstacles, is constantly discussed; consciousness raising is made possible by communications raising.

Identity

Small groups are always in search of their identity, of what they should be called, how they should be described, and how they should be explained to those outside the group. As the search goes on for that elusive identity, there is the recognition that when and if found it will still remain fluid and a work in progress. And it has to be that way because the final shape of the group overlaps the future and is therefore permanently unfinished. Its members will stubbornly refuse to jettison evolution for premature clarity. And yet for all the uncertainty and temporariness of its identity, the difference is clear to everyone involved. And so no one is frantic.

Questioning

The dominant mode of conversation and conducting business is inquiry. Questioning is the norm. Challenging assumptions becomes second nature. Everything is up for grabs. Nothing is sacred. Members regularly unlearn as their version of the learning organization. Innovation is pursued relentlessly, and the sign of its visiting the group is the sense that the future has visited the present.

Autonomy

The group is self-possessed. It is capable of functioning primarily in an open rather than a closed system. Such a system requires that processes constantly be repaired and altered. All design, no matter initially how good and serviceable, is temporary. Unlike mechanical closed systems, which seek perfection because they were designed never to require transformation, the group is constantly self-organizing, self-learning, and self-developing. Autonomy is their version of freedom.

Consensual Culture

Unlike the other items above, this is newly minted. It never existed before in precisely the way it does for each group. It is its signature. It is its modus operandi. It is the way the group evolves to work together with each other as individuals and as a group. It also subsumes all the above. It is created and maintained by communication. The nature of the consensuality constitutes the group's identity and diversity. It evolves and is shaped by the questioning mode. And it is inconceivable without self-organizing systems. In fact, one can claim that consensual cultures are actually the unique creations of such autonomous open systems.

All this is by the way of dramatizing the emergence of teams as the new companion of leadership—as its partner and alter ego—and the new requirement that CEOs embody the cultural leadership of teams. A CEO must occupy the middle ground between independence and interdependence. Granted freedom and autonomy, such heterogeneous cohorts can optimally tap the unlimited potential of diversity and innovation. Freed of the structure and culture of bigness, they are free to create and nourish their own systems organically from within. But to appreciate more fully the impact of teams on leaders, we have to study them more closely.

Quietly, without bravado or fanfare, a new way of working together, problem solving, generating innovations, and aligning mission and vision gradually has worked its way to the center of organizational success. Failure has been averted, direction established, dysfunctional inadequacies addressed, and companies have prospered. Initially small or occasional, teams grew in number, frequency, and range to become now a dominant culture—to the point where simultaneously they function as both hub and cutting edge, microcosm and macrocosm.

But how did it happen so quickly and totally? There were no executive fiats proclaiming from on high, "Let there be teams everywhere!" No vice president was appointed head of all teams. To be sure, HR has always stressed recruiting team players—but that is nothing new. Of course, the training of teams in conflict management and resolution was tireless and insistent but again that was not separate from the general commitment to improving interpersonal relationships. No, if we are to appreciate the current centrality of teams and the extent to which teams rule, we have to step back and look at the capacity of teams not only to dominate but also to be the big picture.

Below are five ways teams uniquely capture and celebrate the essentials of every organization and ensure the quality and performance of its growth.

Leadership

As a training ground for the identification and development of new leaders, nothing matches the laboratory of a team environment. Indeed, its inevitable competition with the official in-house executive leadership development program is generally unacknowledged—a sad linkage lost. Moreover, in a number of ways team leadership is different. First, it is multiple. It is not limited to one official professional, so named and fixed at the top. It is egoless, generic, and ongoing; the baton is passed without ceremony. At its best it is horizontal and embodies the promise of integrated thought and cross-over opportunities. In short, team leadership in essence is distributed. It is shared. Every team leader potentially is an Indian chief.

Rotational

Teams uniquely embrace the notion of rotational leadership as a leadership model. Again situational reality, not pecking order or a fixed spot on the organizational chart, drives who is in charge. In many ways it reenacts the principle of the Roman legion—*primus inter pares*, or first among equals. All are equal; all can command. What determines choice is a reality check and match—who is best able to lead given the challenge, resources, and timetable? And when that task changes so does the leader. Rotational leadership is thus designed to be temporary and to optimize the alignment of talent and task.

Ownership

Team ownership is special. Whatever the charge from without, it is aggressively and officially claimed by the team charter. Each team at the outset produces a collaborative document that in effect is a team governance contract. It spells out the charge, sets up team goals in stages, and identifies the roles of each team member. Nothing is left to chance. Everything is included. It is totally self-directed and administered. Above all, each team functions as the company in miniature, with collaborative solutions contingent upon the degree to which the problem is collectively owned. Indeed, many professionals flourish more in team environments than as solos, and, if ways can be found to identify those people in advance, teams would start off with one leg up.

Diversity

Teams confront diversity constantly and transform enemies into allies, obstacles into enrichment. Increasingly functioning in a global world and economy, virtual teams have become the norm and have had to optimize diversity as the state of the art. What is often not fully appreciated is the extent to which virtual teams replace singularity of disciplines with that of a mosaic. In the process, they have created unique knowledge intersects and cross-overs.

Root Self-Definition and Cause

The team ideal is Kaizen—the pursuit of root cause. In this case, however, it is applied also to the solution. The team shifts into operational mode to determine the extent to which the solution when implemented may be a problem. Such forethought is supported by another team requirement. The special strengths of each member are not a mystery but a known quantity. His quadrant has been tested and identified, and we know in advance what he is good at and how the facets of his personality best interface with that of others. The net result is that a typical team miniaturizes the operations and culture of the company and what can jeopardize implementation.

In addition, other benefits might be as follows:

- Measurable increase in customer satisfaction
- Faster decisions
- Problems resolved at the source
- Prevailing harmony
- High morale
- Low absenteeism

All that is required is a small revolution. For all of the above to happen, management has to give up control and CEOs have to lead less.

Leadership Challenges of Age—Seven Deadly Sins

5

AGING AND DISEASE ARE ROUTINELY PAIRED. The latter typically has dominated medical research. That is understandable: disease is urgent, marketable, and hopefully treatable. Thus, procedures and medications focused on the disease side of the equation successfully have halted or slowed the three great killers and debilitators: heart disease, stroke, and cancer. But recently the question of the cause and effect relationship between aging and disease has been raised and a new answer has been forthcoming.

Dr. Aubrey de Grey of Cambridge recently turned around the linkage of age and disease. He argued that aging itself was the villain of the piece, and then went on to identify its seven deadly ways of prematurely doing us in. In other words, the focus on the diseases associated with aging should be altered to the overall disease of aging itself. That shifts attention away from the impact on the branches to the root of the problem.

De Grey's argument is persuasive because both his starting and end points—cellular health—are not only totally inclusive but also not limited to age. Disease resulting from cell debilitation can occur at any time in the life cycle. There are research hospitals devoted to cancer in children. Furthermore, focusing on aging provides a number of vantage points:

1. Aging provides the most dramatically pervasive description of cellular degeneration.
2. It also identifies the many cross-overs from aging to disease.
3. It sets up a systemic blueprint for future research.
4. Specifically, it calls for a body-wide bioremediation program using stem cell and gene therapy to halt or delay what aging causes.
5. Finally, it nicely accommodates genetic research, including cognitive findings, as DNA triggers many of the cellular problems.

What also may be attractive is the prospect of using de Grey's perspective as a metaphor to apply to the body politic. To what extent do governments, societies, and organizations show signs of aging irrespective of the chronological composite or census? Is it possible to translate cellular degeneration into organizational equivalents and apply those to businesses? Would such an overlay and process produce a diagnostic profile of the health of an organization and to what extent it is suffering from any or all of the seven deadly ailments?

The list below describes each deadly sign as a specific medical problem followed by its application as a business equivalent.

Too Few New Cells

Problem: Certain body systems lose their ability to renew their cells, resulting in loss of muscle tone, brain cells, and bone.

Application: Many organizations unknowingly cut themselves off from future self-renewal. They hire and promote personnel only from the same colleges and parts of the country or only from the United States. Those at the top are routinely male and monochromatic. Most serious of all, training is reassuring, not renewing. It affirms but does not disturb the basic culture. The result often is flabby, predictable, and brittle thinking.

Too Many Old and Harmful Cells

Problem: Cells no longer divide as they should. They refuse to die but secrete toxic poisons.

Application: Many organizational visions and missions no longer shake and stir. The bibliography of leaders and managers often ends with their graduation dates. Most of their ideas are so tried and tested that they are old and tired. Everyone is on Geritol. Even R&D does not value or read science fiction. And they all obediently sign up for the same old conferences. The grim joke applies: dead at forty, buried at eighty.

DNA Mutations in the Cell Nucleus

Problem: The control mechanism of the DNA breaks down or malfunctions. The cancer it causes is so endemic and inaccessible that it is extremely difficult to reach or treat.

Application: What constitutes the DNA of an organization? Its brains and smarts? The cortex has been called the CEO of the brain. What does it direct and shape? If the characteristic answer is always or only leadership at the top, the company may be vulnerable. The correct antidote probably should be company-wide. Distributed or shared leadership multiples the source and diversity of DNA. Paradoxically, the less control, the more coordination there is; the less dependency, the more independence.

Muting of Energy Generators

Problem: Mitochondria are the body's energy generators and age to the point where vigor is diminished or lost entirely. Parkinson's may be one of its signs.

Application: Who and what generates a company's energy? Where are its energy centers? What is its energy profile? Many organizations are listless. They just grind and drag along. There are no highs or lows, just a deadly even pace. They are boring. And their plans and decision-making process are generally timid and tentative. Both their thinking and their hands shake.

Clogging Cell Waste

Problem: Many cells lose their ability to break down and dispose of their own waste. Gradually, the waste accumulates and clogs vital systems and degeneration of various kinds occurs.

Application: Many organizations have not only dead wood, but also dead ideas. They have no systematic mechanism for regularly identifying and cleaning out such waste. They limp along carrying excess weight and baggage that they should routinely and regularly be rid of. In short, if no one in the organization is in charge of regular intellectual trash disposal, it will gradually accumulate and choke off function.

Between Cells

Problem: The waste between cells gathers and forms globs of gunk impairing brain and liver functions.

Applications: Often the productivity problems within divisions are nothing compared to those between them. Carry-over or shared tasks frequently fall between the proverbial cracks. Managers are not so much in charge of, as locked into, divisions. The results they produce are always solely divisional. But who oversees divisional connectivity? Who claims interdivisional gains? Who clears and cleans the passages between cells and divisions?

Proteins Sticking Together

Problem: Structural molecules cling excessively together and clog and harden arteries.

Application: Certain structures and ideas have an affinity for each other. They bind and cluster. If they gain majority they become company culture. Comfort is thus cloned and thinking alike becomes the reassuring norm. There is no disagreement or friction. Everyone becomes a ball bearing. The argument of aging, however, is that no single aggregate or binder, no matter how initially appropriate or enlivening, is healthy. All needs to be free flowing, changing, and constantly circulating. Clogging is what obstructs company change and reengineering.

In summary, then, what are the benefits of examining the causes of organizational aging? There are at least five:

1. It is diagnostic and thus corrective.
2. It is total: it fuses the physiological and the psychological, the body and the mind, inborn and acquired behaviors.
3. It is holistic: it bypasses the reductive choices of nature versus nurture and makes them instead versions of and avenues to each other.
4. It is self-administered: each organization can assess itself by undergoing minimally an annual aging check up.
5. It profiles: it sets up the key diagnostic questions to ask and to evaluate as a critical checklist.

But securing the benefits above requires a systematic diagnostic process that reflects the organizational versions of the seven deadly sins:

Diagnostic Profile of Organizational Aging

Annual Check-Up Checklist

1. To what extent are we a self-renewing company?
2. Are we coasting on past health and capacity?
3. What constitutes our DNA and how well does it direct and manage?
4. What is the company's energy level?
5. Any dead wood and ideas around?
6. What is the traffic between divisions?
7. What is the capacity to clean house and get rid of cumulative waste?

Table 5.1. Aging Behaviors and Changes Needed

Focus	Aging Behaviors	Correctives
1. Self-Renewal	Homogeneous	Diverse
2. Past-Oriented	Tenured Ideas	Futuristic
3. Dominating DNA	Singular Tunnel Vision	Holistics
4. Energy Level	Uneven	Untapped
5. Deadwood/Ideas	Micro-Managed	Big Picture
6. Communication	Occasional	Ongoing
7. Clogging	Choking Structures	Fluidity

Table 5.2. Thinking, Learning, and Leading Applications

1. Self-Renewal	Linear Sequential	Circular
2. Ideas	Unexamined Assumptions	Square One Basics
3. Genetics	Deterministic	Nature/Nurture Symbiosis
4. Energy/Drive	Top Heavy	Distributed and Diffused
5. Clearing the field	Excess Baggage	Change as Innovation
6. Conversations	Muted and Limited	Free-Flowing
7. Thinking	Predictable	Unexpected

Such overlays, distributed perhaps as a survey internally to employees and externally to customers (coded to identify the source but not name), may generate a profile of the degree to which the entire company is a senior citizen and a number of its parts should be retired. But whatever is portrayed, the process not only serves as a wake-up call but also identifies corrective action. As such, it thus can generate both the immediate and long-term future agenda of the organization and even perhaps not just project but also protect its longevity. But, as discussed in the next chapter, what about the role of followers?

Leadership and Empowerment   **6**

Stealing people's decisions is wrong.

—CHARLES HANDY, *BEYOND CERTAINTY* (1996)

HAPPILY, THE SINGULAR HOMOGENEITY of corporations no longer exists. In its place, there is incredible diversity—of employees, divisions, structures, multinational operations, alliances, partners, acquisitions, and mergers. In short, a whole host of different cultures currently coexists. The quest for corporate unity therefore routinely encounters the patchwork quilt of the United States and even more so now that of the global market. And yet the search for such unity is a job requirement for CEOs and managers.

It is an awesome, recurrent, and relentless task at which, alas, more often than not, managers falter and fail. They may have a better chance of success, however, if the following guidelines are heeded:

1. Commonality and unity are not the same. They also are not equally valued. Although initially unknown and unavailable, commonality is discoverable.
2. The energy of the apex and the middle derives from the base. Inquiry of common purpose should follow reverse delegation.
3. Power resides in and belongs to the lowest point of the organization.

4. Managers, and not CEOs, are positioned for optimum access and definition.
5. The secrets of commonality may be more discoverable and accessible with employee participation and involvement.
6. Such bottom-up contributions always should pursue internal alignment with company objectives.
7. Managerial guidance structures such alignment and priorities congruence.

The focus of managers is therefore clear: to discover what holds their units together as the avenue to what holds the company together. It is critical at the divisional level where it has to happen and where there is also sufficient diversity to test comprehensive applicability. In the process, the manager has to share the leadership of his task with the employees of his unit if the search for commonality is to become both generic and diverse and, thus, both applicable and adaptable to all other units. Involving all and undertaken across the board, the discovery of commonality may be consensual.

The temptation is to limit the search to known or identifiable weak or soft spots suffering from a lack of common purpose. But that may be deceptive or distractive—a fast and dirty focus. Better to be comprehensive and archetypal. Miniaturize the search to organizational essentials: mission, future planning, employee demographics, leadership, and training.

Mission

Mission is listed first because obviously that is where common purpose is expressed. But how obvious is it really? And how well does it serve as a nexus? Two extremes dominate: many companies have not revisited their mission statements for years; others seem to do it every week. In addition, the review process itself may be exclusively the province of senior officers and thus not really serve the cause of diverse corrective revision. The CEO and his senior staff may shuffle words around or jazz it up with the latest buzzwords, but it may still emerge as the same tired, interchangeable, and predictable statement that could apply to many companies. The pressure of commonality compels that another and more basic source of mission be found.

A number of organizations have been experimenting with employee mission statements (EMSs). In its basic form, managers ask employees individually to identify their job parts in the form of a mission statement. They subsequently designate how their performance will be measured. Then, because each employee shares that job description with others doing the same job, the next phase involves developing a master EMS of all those job parts and measures common to the same job. "I" at that point changes to "we," an important symbolic inclusion and change. The net result is a collective template and identity, cutting across different divisions, sites, and even countries, of occupational identities and goals.

The third phase seeks to assign priorities to each EMS and its parts, but this phase is negotiated and not determined unilaterally. What fixes the priorities are the overall business goals of the corporation. Employees with their supervisors select those job activities, goals, and measures that serve best to accomplish those business goals. Thus, employee missions are aligned with the company's mission.

The company mission statement now becomes an aggregated core of common employee mission statements. Every individual and every group of job-specific individuals—indeed, every employee in the company—is welded together to articulate and share a common purpose and focus. The alignment of priorities clinches the process by creating a nexus between top and bottom. The flow of the organization cascades downwards and ascends upwards. The functions of the organization now can move more easily from the vertical to the horizontal as work and goal commonality emerges.

Future Planning

One of the most effective ways of determining whether everyone is on the same page is to identify a common challenge or opportunity, especially in the future. But again that can serve as a rallying point only if all are genuinely invited to face it together. It cannot remain a monopoly of the CEO and the senior staff or strategic planners. In other words, like the EMS process itself, it must be comprehensively participatory. In fact, that EMS can be used as a future probe.

Some managers experimenting with EMS have pushed the envelope further. Having compiled a current version of an EMS as the benchmark, employees then have been asked to create an aspirational version that incorporates and factors in skills and attributes to be acquired, especially in light of future challenges. The yields from this exercise are equally and impressively multiple. Most obviously, the workforce becomes future directed, even future driven. A comparison of the current with the future version quickly yields the training agenda needed to get from here to there. Finally, if a company wishes to capture the momentum of such a collective effort and render it with greater precision, employees already are primed and receptive to participate in an environmental scanning process that, buttressed by books, articles, and speakers, can shape and create an in-house, company-wide, employee futures collective. Such anticipatory commonality would produce a projection of decision alternatives, which might model perfectly the future core of the company itself.

Employee Demographics and Diversity

Currently, at least five, soon to be six, generations coexist in a large organization. The earliest were born in the 1940s and the latest in the 1980s, with the range of their retirement running from 2025 to 2065. Nearly fifty years of history span and determine the five cohorts and display their different and often conflicting value systems.

Of late that has been compounded by companies forming overseas alliances with cultures that are often at variance with some basic American drives. Software programmers from India, for example, employed by American companies do not seem to be as comfortable with the challenge of initiative and opportunity as their American counterparts. Instead, they would prefer decisions to be already made and tasks to be assigned by others. In short, how is commonality to be found in the midst of such diversity?

Discovering common denominators may involve valuing paradox or ambiguity rather than an either/or attitude. For example, extremes are often posed as false alternatives: everybody is the same or everybody is different. Typically, people are invited to choose one or the other position. The truth of paradox is that everybody is the same, differently. The commonality of sameness offers a common core for understanding, action, and communication.

Co-Leadership

Discovering commonality ultimately rests on leadership sharing. Indeed, to a large extent leadership itself is a source of commonality but only when it is parceled out, even multiplied, and is no longer a monopoly of the top. Transactional leaders at different times, for different reasons, and with different tweaks, have endorsed distributed leadership as a company-wide empowerment strategy.

For Robert Greenleaf, distributed leadership takes two forms. First, it extends servant leadership across all decision points. Everyone thus would serve first and lead second. It also transfers leadership ultimately and selflessly to the organization rather than imprisoning leadership within the executive superstructure. Distributing leadership among all employees and even writing it into all job descriptions would not require everyone to exercise leadership whenever and wherever it presented itself. Clients found that such shared or common leadership enervated the company, generated creativity, and identified future leaders for promotion.

Finally, in a completely different area, that of public education, Richard Elmore sought to address the situation of principals routinely being overwhelmed by the demands of the job as well as the increasing shortage of new educational administrators. His solution was to call for distributing the leadership horizontally to all teachers and professional staff so as to create a more manageable, accountable, and productive structure. In the process, what emerged increasingly as a new source of commonality was the teacher-leader comparable to the middle-level manager. But these teacher-leaders remained in the classroom. In the process, they uniquely embodied the integration of administration, instruction, and measurement.

Training

This final item returns the discussion to where it started. When employees are asked to compose their own mission statement followed by the increasingly inclusive process across the company, and when further future sights are raised and incorporated, what is produced is the commonality of shared purpose. In addition, that happily is not an abstract or imprecise understanding but one that is rooted in the specifics of every job each person does. But perhaps its most powerful expression is the common desire to be more than they currently are.

When the expression of personal potential is extended horizontally and transferred vertically from the base to the apex, and when leadership is shared and diversity valued, both commonality and the future become the nexus and mission of the company.

Discovering and nurturing such aspirations programs the company's future. Training and development then is harnessed on behalf of commonality of potential. Specifically, the training must incorporate the commonalties discovered. Thus, the training agenda itself should not be determined unilaterally but collaboratively, not from on high but from rank-and-file needs and aspirations. Training also should not be limited to incremental updates, but should anticipate future developments. Harvesting company-wide identification and evaluation of trends should be a training objective, just as developing distributed leadership should be supported by training exercises. Above all, a major thrust of training should be stirring innovation. For such creative outcomes to involve everyone, all efforts need to ride the coattails of distributed leadership and benefit from the diversity of different people doing the same things differently.

What is perhaps now clear is that the search for commonality is inevitably reinforcing. It is a circular process. Each of the five areas above increasingly becomes interactively aligned. The orbits of leadership and diversity overlap and together they both support new ideas and future creativity. The net result is an organization structurally more like a network than a pyramid, more interconnected than separate, and more multiple than singular; it is steered in one common direction, even though thousands are at the helm. Finally, the commonality shared is one of transactional empowerment (see table 6.1).

Table 6.1.   Empowerment Matrix

Categories	Before Empowerment	After Empowerment
1. Structure	Centralized (Vertical)	Decentralized (Horizontal)
2. Job Description	Prescribed	Self-Directed
3. Mission Statement	Organizational	Employee
4. Operations	Function	Process
5. Employees	Workers	Assets
6. Leadership	Specified (Top-Down)	Distributed (Available)
7. Pay	Salary	Gains-Sharing
8. Human Resources	Recruitment	Retention
9. Relationships	Individual (Independence)	Group (Interdependence)
10. Training	Homogeneous (Singular)	Heterogeneous (Cross-Divisional)
11. Information	Hoarded	Shared
12. Performance	Blame/Shame	Improvement
13. Manager	Boss	Coach
14. Listening	Limited/Selective	Feedback/Feed Forward
15. Decisions	Top-Down	Consensual
16. Innovation	R&D	Learning Organization
17. Forecasting	Planners	Lay Forecasting
18. Agreements	Contracts	Covenants
19. Voice	Singular	Multiple
20. Roles	Given	Negotiated

Followers as SOBs 7

I T IS PROBABLY POLITICALLY INCORRECT to endorse obsession. This is especially true now, when many urge balance between work and family, between matters of the spirit and the bottom line, between being a kindly coach and a forceful leader. But professionals are working harder and longer hours than ever before. Besides, boards favor organizations that are vision driven, future driven, and leader driven. Driven is not exactly non-obsessive. The proverbial quest for fame and fortune has never been more realizable. More new millionaires and billionaires were created in this last decade than in the entire twentieth century

If such behavior is encouraged and even sanctioned, it seems somewhat hypocritical and yet understandable for organizations to hold aloft the image of the non-excessive manager. No company wants to acknowledge that under the velvet glove there is an iron fist. Perhaps the wisest course is to find a model that at least somewhat redeems or softens the edge of that drive and yet maintains its ruthlessly singular and intense focus. One recommendation is to apply a phrase often repeated, invoked, and urged: become a student of the business (SOB).

SOB often unambiguously describes a manager who compulsively lives, eats, and breathes the business and in the process may have developed uncanny instincts for what is central and futuristic. Warren Bennis relates a confession of Ben Rick of Lockheed Martin: "I always know a good idea when I hear it, because of the feeling of terror that seizes me." Rick was describing two students of the business: the one who always searches for that piercing idea and the other who has it. What are the characteristics and qualities of a student of the business? What distinguishes that special state from the conventional knowledge worker? And how do such followers impact leaders?

SOBs evidence at least five obsessive qualities: instinct, self-learning, convictions, endless inquiry, and problem solving.

Instinct

The SOB has an ear and a nose for what is genuinely new, even groundbreaking. Students of the business develop instincts, hunches, and feelings; they have highly developed antennae. But such reliance on intuition is not merely an early warning and opportunity system—although it can significantly function that way. Above all, it is a way of knowing. They can ferret out something about to disturb the universe. Like Rick, they do not have to be the one doing it. Their obsession is initially to recognize it, then to give it credence, and finally perhaps to lure it into this world. Like collectors of anything—pens, spittoons, stamps, coins—students of the business are always looking for the rare gem, for the holy grail.

Self-Learning

Formal education often has little to do with the process. In fact, it can be an obstacle. MBAs may be more imprisoning than liberating. The SOB develops his own favorite way of seeking and acquiring knowledge—his own curriculum. But the respect for insight is total and pivotal. Unexpected "eurekas" can set the SOB off on a life journey.

A teacher or colleague may embody a kind of endlessly probing curiosity that is seminal and stirring. A student may ask a question that comes out of nowhere, does not follow the familiar trajectory, and further is inimitable because that student is wired that way. A book or an article may stop the SOB in his tracks and rapidly become a personal bible. Or an opportunity to do some original research may result in being bitten by the bug of discovery. And if that happens again and again and lasts, one is permanently possessed.

Convictions

The problem is that, although the above experiences may happen to many, they come to naught mostly because of fear—of being perceived as uncompromising, the intimidation of conventional company culture, and the paralysis of taking risks. Many are more comfortable on the sidelines cheering the obsessives on to oblivion. Indeed, such intense SOBs are often condescendingly advised that, if they want to get ahead and be accepted, they ought to toe the mark. Conventional "wisdom" is pushed again and again at every stage until most buckle and begin to love their captors and slavery. But convictions dictate otherwise and preserve persistence and singular integrity. After a while the genuine SOB realizes that his strength and difference are part and parcel of his very identity—they are who he is. More than two hundred years ago, William Blake proclaimed, "I must create my own system or be enslaved by another's."

Endless Inquiry

Such types also are endless probers. They never stop asking questions. They are reminiscent of Louis B. Mayer's classic statement: "For your information, let me ask you a question." They are relentless. They get the scent and are off like Sherlock Holmes, pursuing the mystery until it gives up the ghost. They are often boring and even pedantic. They always start conversations with "Did you know . . . ?" They are capable of ruining dinner parties or being brushed off and told to get a life. But nothing stops or slows them down. They shake those comments off and look for another victim. Although they may be tiresome to others, they are never bored with themselves. They cover the waterfront and never miss very much if anything. Pedantry aside, they frequently find shortcuts to the basics or circuitous approaches to the center. A student of the business is searching for the impossible, which he secretly hopes he will never find because it is the search, not the end prize, that stirs him.

Problem Solver

He is an inveterate problem solver, an admirer of those who pull rabbits out of hats, and tireless seeker of the state of the art. One could not find a better champion of innovation and creativity. What he finds particularly creative are new theories and metaphors that force reformulation, that require the entire world to be viewed differently. Such insights approach revelation. He operates on the assumption that nothing is known forever, and that knowledge will be overturned regularly and without warning. Finally, he is a major advocate for the future, which he believes will be incredible and beyond present imagination. Ultimately, all students of the business seek to approach the threshold of time, to know all that can be known up to that point, and then to gaze and search for the new, the dazzling, and what has not yet been thought of. They all read science fiction and compose scenarios.

In short what does this obsessive managerial model of the student of the business offer managers and leaders and confer on their organizations? At least five benefits. First, it urges managers and leaders to think back to a time and place and person that compelled them to be obsessive—when they underwent an all-nighter not because they were cramming but rather totally possessed; when they did not so much decide to write something but rather it selected them to write it; when they were possessed by an idea or a vision that they could not let go of and that gave them no peace; and finally when they thought of going into business for themselves or actually created such a business, for all obsessives are entrepreneurial. Such experiences minimally will establish a basis for identification and kinship and enable managers to contemplate as a real future a mode of operation that is not totally unfamiliar or unattractive.

Second, the model of the student of the business can be used to assess and examine the degree of complacency and comfort of managers. How much is routine, how much is accepted as absolute gospel that will never change, and how much inertia is built into the company culture? Is the organization driven to possess a future unique and discontinuous from everyone else in the industry? In short, is the organizational culture itself a student of the business?

Third, it compels probing and dislocating questions to be asked. Have any been raised at meetings, in teams, in formulating policy and planning? Are challenging questions and analysis generally rated highly and viewed favorably? Is the culture a questioning or pacifying culture, risking little, playing it safe, always being predictable?

Fourth, does the organization settle too quickly for answers or solutions? Is everything solved with the same solution system or tool kit? When was the last time anyone pushed the question or issue harder, beyond conventional wisdom and familiar thresholds? Is the environment placid or passionate? Are there any resident madmen, idea lunatics, or obsessive searchers?

Finally, has everyone been reading the same business books? Are they ever discussed? Put on the agenda for a meeting? They all can't be right, can they? Where's the synthesis? Who are the company's innovators? Are they recognized and rewarded? How is creativity and futurity tied together? How many students of the business does the organization have?

Imagine a CEO who could boast, "My managers generally are all obsessives. They are all SOBs." And, as noted in the next chapter, they are also occupied with the big picture.

Holistics: Managers versus Leaders　　8

A KEY DISCIPLINE FOR FINDING A COMPANY'S animating energy is holistics. Why is holistics so adept at this deep task? Does it perform as an organizational psychiatrist or archeologist? What is it?

Holistics is a process of comprehensive inquiry. It encircles a subject, taps the full reach of its implications, and reaches beyond the predictably known. It delays analysis, often viewing it as prematurely reductive. It is not disdainful of data but is not driven by it either. It assumes that what is being searched for is not yet available for quantification. In short, it is a mode of inquiry, a process of organizational soul searching.

It is not done once and for all time and then memorialized in a vision statement. It is up for grabs daily whenever problems have to be solved and a future action has to be chosen. In a real and active sense it is the threshold for planning, innovation, and reinvention. It must always obey a basic law. It must never become too theoretical or removed from daily operations.

The method to its macro-reach is invariably circular and entwining and involves three steps. The first involves stepping back, the second stepping aside, and the third stepping ahead. The holistic process is the art of seeing things whole—stepping back to see the forest as well as the trees. It is also the art of seeing things that are directly threatening or compromising—stepping aside to see dangers. And finally it is the art of anticipating the future—stepping ahead to see the unforeseeable.

The three-step system is tyrannical in that it requires that the three steps be completed every time the holistic process is invoked. Although the order is not sacred, there can't be any fast and dirty shortcuts. What follows below is an elaboration of each step followed by an application of holistics to managerial decision-making.

Stepping Back

The art of seeing things whole is harder than it sounds because it is always somewhat mysterious. Like the proverbial tip of the iceberg, every event or opportunity involves more than meets the eye. Thus, the prospect of a new market may be enticing but the totality of that market may be greater or different than initially appears. The methodology of technology assessment may be particularly helpful here.

What is the first, second, third, fourth, and fifth order of impact of the technology being introduced? The durability of each order of impact, as well as the probability of spinning off other technologies, are all part of the ever-widening process of approximating the whole and of achieving a grasp of the macro-reach of the market prior to entering it.

It is probably unfair to lord it over those in the past who minimized the whole and thus underestimated its extent. But what such short-sightedness underscores is the absence of holistics, which compulsively is always more inclusive. Holistics takes off and goes beyond where others have stopped. The assumption of premature mastery, of having plumbed the depths, is usually the infallible sign that we have sold our intelligence and organizations short.

The articulation and analysis of unacknowledged assumptions is the special focus of holistics. Similarly, sizing up the competition is often partial and self-indulgent. Seldom, if ever, is there an assessment of the talent of our competitors. Planners sometimes do not even know anything about their counterparts in competing companies—where they went to school, what their track record is, what risk management tolerances they employ, and so forth. Then, too, often there is little or no discussion of who else is thinking the way we are. Most often that is limited to who else is not planning or doing things the way we are.

Patiently, then, as stepping back and back further proceeds, the whole, or much more than what a partial or constrained range of inquiry generally yields, begins to emerge. More and more of the iceberg is exposed; the opportunity becomes increasingly three-dimensional. It becomes the table of contents of a total story. It is no longer an idea but a full-fledged scenario. It appears to have all the realism and clarity of animated ideas and opportunities. But it is not finished. It is poised for possible revision.

Stepping Aside

If the first step is thesis, the second step is antithesis. So many plays and films produced somehow seem to have successfully avoided any encounter with sobering reality. So many ventures and new businesses are based on heady expectations but have no sense of gravity. So many careers are fast tracked to oblivion.

One must step aside so as to see where and when the road may unpredictably veer dangerously off the main path. In short, there is a need to be failure oriented, to hearken to naysayers and the "yes, but" types—in short, to encourage the loyal and even disloyal opposition. But again it must be holistic in scope.

It cannot be on a scale smaller than the projected venture itself. That would be deceptive. And even when safeguards and adjustments have been made, monitoring has to join planning as an equal and permanent partner. The venture must never be allowed to become uncritically self-perpetuating or self-directing, especially if it appears to promise success. Thesis has to match antithesis totally in substance, toughness, and scale. We have to worry as much as we dream.

Stepping Ahead

But isn't the third step of anticipation—stepping ahead—superfluous or out of order? No, because forecasting is the ultimate check and balance. It comes from another place and time. It has not yet been centrally tapped. It is not part of the original critical apparatus. It is a new player. And it will make or break all that has preceded so far. Its voice is special because it fuses analysis and intuition.

The future is a mixture of the known, the unknown, and the unknowable. We already know a great deal about the future through the extrapolation of demographics and known resources. The unknown is not unknowable. It is available as trends, long-term cycles, various predictors of systems behaviors, and so forth. All of these can be tapped and factored into the building up of the original totality. They contribute to the antithesis. But the future is also finally unknowable—that is the way in fact the future remains the future. Nevertheless, it is foreseeable; it can be imagined. Utopian, dystopian, and science-fiction writers have been doing it for centuries with remarkably accurate results.

The final step then is to step ahead of the known and the unknown to sense the direction of the unknowable—to try to provide the thesis and antithesis with a future in the form of an intuitive synthesis. This final act, however, is not discontinuous with the two impulses that have shaped this realistic and imaginative whole in the first place. The future compels further, albeit more speculative, consideration of totality as well as its future threats. Above all, it adds a dimension currently missing: the future of the future.

So many organizations and managers assume a friendly future. It will agreeably accommodate their planning and thinking. It will always affirm and never question the direction of the totality they have assembled and even the perils. But until and unless one seeks that final reach, no matter how tenuously, the art of holistics is not complete, and the gift of wholeness, contingency, and speculation that it confers upon organizations, planners, and forecasters may be less than generous, enlarging, and bracing. Indeed, that sin of omission may be the ultimate peril.

The value of holistics thus lies in its straddling of opposites—vision and reality, utopia and dystopia. Its correctives are enormous. It brings assumptions to the level of conscious examination. It fixes a quizzical and tough eye on cherished definitions and sacred cows. It requires that the art of conceptualization flirt with intuition, and compels vision to be savvy. Above all, at a minimum holistics should make uncertainty more manageable and success more achievable and both permanently incomplete.

The final step is always application, but in this case it also involves disseminating holistics throughout the organization and involving the rank and file in the process. The kind of people we are looking for in our management ranks is someone who can be persuasive and who can also make people cooperate with them. Management is not dictatorship. "A company will get nowhere if all the thinking is left to management. Everybody in the company must contribute their minds" (Akio Morita, *Made in Japan* [1986]).

A significant way of measuring such change or its absence is examining the way managers manage. The options for managing employees and for employees managing themselves have increased significantly. Not surprisingly, so have the ways of communicating managing. In fact, the two often are linked. There are at least three major directionally driven managerial models: the vertical, the horizontal, and the circular. Each is paired with an appropriate communication partner.

There is the traditional directive style of telling workers what to do and how to do it. This is basically a top-down singular style of perfection because there is implicitly only one way to do it. The supervisor, like the proverbial version of "Father knows best," always has the right answer. Often such paternalism works well, and the path prescribed frequently is in fact the best one to follow. But that method requires nearly total vertical obedience to the chain or command, on the one hand, and faith in the paternal wisdom and goodness of a boss, on the other hand.

Hardly ever is the question asked why this is being done or whether this is the best or only way. Managers generally know why and share it with other managers—that is the official and inside talk between managers—but not with employees. Occasionally, the why may be used as a trump card to eliminate disobedience or mild mutiny. Finally, the dominant communications mode is prescriptive. Following the military models, orders are given.

Another method is coaching or facilitating. The directive has been replaced by a question and answer system. In some cases, it also may incorporate the Japanese ritual of asking the question "Why?" at least five times when a problem arises in order to get at the root cause. Applied horizontally and company wide, it is particularly effective when the company also commits itself to being a questioning and communicating culture.

At the heart of this method is dialogue. The degree to which conversation is employed and what areas it covers varies with the security or insecurity of the manager. Supervisors, who are determined to retain control and still be directive, will be reluctant to share all or too much lest it undermine their superior position. Titles and egos are intertwined. Still, even a fifty-fifty mixture of the directive and coaching styles usually creates efficiency, sustains morale, and builds communication bridges better than the totally directive approach.

The third mode is circular. It is the most ambitious and complex. It has a number of subsets and is potentially the most robust and most demanding of both managers and employees. The key variable is the degree to which managers are indispensable, dispensable, and finally invisible or nearly absorbed as co-leaders. The progress through these three stages has as its ultimate goal the manager's responsibility to create and communicate an employee-centered culture.

It might be helpful at this point to summarize in matrix form the three basic styles and then to identify the subsets of the third managerial one for further exploration (see table 8.1).

Table 8.2 identifies the three progressive subsets of management development, which increasingly involve employee participation to the point where they become co-managers.

Table 8.1.   Managerial Style Matrix

Managerial Style	Direction	Communication Mode	Outcomes
1. Directive	Vertical	Prescriptive	Predictive/Singular
2. Coaching	Horizontal	Suggestive	Multiple
3. Team Leader	Circular	Dialogue	Collective

Table 8.2.   Management Development

Leader Roles	Communication Modes	Outcomes
1. Manager as Team Leader/Coach	Directive and Dialogue Exchange	Guided Solutions and Limited Creativity
2. Manager as Consultant	Suggestive	Guided Change
3. Manager-Employee Shared Leadership	Circular Exchange	Innovation

Shared Leadership

The first version is a transitional hybrid. The managerial role softens, becomes less overbearing and confrontational, and employs a more oblique approach. The manager still holds forth a great deal, moralizes and sermonizes sometimes, but he also listens. His favorite summary question is no longer "Anyone not know what he has to do?" but rather "Have we heard from everyone at this point?"

The solutions generated still bear the mark of the manager and his preferred way of doing things. But employee input broadens the range of the discussion and helps to make more visible and important the relationship between divisions and between employees and senior management. The latter sometimes discomfits the manager. The tune that goes through his mind is "How are you going to keep them down on the farm after they have seen Paris?" But he makes sure little or none of that creeps into any written communications. He is sometimes delighted, although surprised, by some of the more creative thinking that takes place.

The second mode requires the manager to inhabit the periphery of the team. He functions as a resource. His style is thus largely consultative. He generally participates only when asked questions, although he often may try to regain his former indispensability. Generally, he is involved in two activities: the need for factual and technical information, and negotiating conflicts between members of the team.

Serving as a broker in conflict resolution is often a new role for managers. In the directive function, disputes are just ordered to stop and that's that. But here the manager has to employ a craft he may not have used before, and which he in fact also may have to learn and master. Managers who develop the difficult style of negotiation and see both the individual and team benefits it yields may in the process discover a managerial dimension that more than compensates for whatever loss of authority they experienced.

In any case, depending less on the insistent style of the manager and more on the pliability and creativity of the team, the solutions generated will be a mixture of the two inputs. It will be somewhat directive, singular, familiar, and even managerially predictable. But if the team is also empowered, and develops a sense of its collective intelligence, the solutions may be more imaginative and robust. The team indeed may begin to sense its difference and even its power to identify alternatives. That happy prospect may be viewed with suspicion and even alarm if the manager believes he is threatened.

In the third or last version, employees share the driver's seat. They basically run and lead the team but they are constrained from taking over totally. After all, managers do not have a monopoly on being the boss. Workers can be just as directive, prescriptive, and arbitrary. Lest that throwback occur, the manager may insist that team leadership at best is temporary and rotational. Who leads varies with the competence required. When the challenge changes, the employee-leader changes. As a result, competence is assured. And the flexibility and security of that rotation by one of their own brings out the best and most creative, out-of-the-box solutions to problems.

At this point the manager, in addition to serving as a consultant in terms of data and conflict resolution, becomes a productive member of the team. As such he may take his turn as team leader if he possesses the particular competence required. If he yearns for the good old days when he was boss, he will not be a happy camper. But if he sees his role as helping to sustain and be an integral part of a shared management environment that contributes significantly to increased productivity, profitability, and performance and brings innovative approaches to problem solving, he may find that it more than compensates for what he may have given up. And in his less stressful and more fulfilled moments, he also may even acknowledge that managers do not have a monopoly on management and are not the only, and even sometimes not the most important, players in the game of thinking, learning, and leading.

The last outcome brings the learning review smack up against the future and the need to anticipate it. It is at this point where what lies ahead generates the unfinished agenda. The evaluation of past solutions or interventions against the realities they were supposed to address may recover and underscore innovative notions or creative problem-solving techniques suggested by managers along the way but which for various reasons never took hold or were tried out.

There is, thus, about this process of future facing, the dimension of leapfrogging—let us catch up while leaping ahead. Standing at the

Janerian threshold where the past and future converge, managers may wish to indulge in the illusion of a blank slate. They may wish to enjoy the luxury of speculating on what a manager and an organization ideally should be in the future, and where both have fallen short in the past. Finally, because these regrets also may be more global than what surfaced in the series of outcomes noted above, they may even be more provocative—that is, appropriately futuristic.

In summary, then, the value of the learning inventory lies in the urgent intelligence that is brought to bear, in raising to the level of conscious review assumptions that drive decisions, and compelling an insightful interplay between the past, the present, and the future. In many ways, it is a structured and revealing mid-life crisis designed to create or restore balance for the future. It generates renewal and recommitment as a more informed and proactive professional. Undertaken company-wide, it can give organizations new transactional vitality, direction, and purpose.

At the end of Mark Twain's *Huck Finn*, our young hero, after reviewing his many escapades, is not content just to hang around and resolves instead "to light out for the territory ahead." For Huck, that was the lure of the West. It was also the promise of the future. For America, it was both. This country has always had a love affair with what lies ahead. Now there is also the need to find ways of reconfiguring the branch points for its managers of the future.

As the next chapter suggests, do not ignore conversations.

LEADERSHIP DEVELOPMENT II

The Conversations of Leaders 9

I N THE FILM *CAST AWAY*, THE CHARACTER Chuck Noland (played by Tom Hanks) finds a volleyball among the debris washed ashore on a deserted island. It looks like a face. He decides to call it Wilson after the manufacturer's name on the ball and proceeds to have regular conversations with Wilson. Clearly, that arrangement saves his sanity. In fact, when he is on his precarious raft trying to find land or a ship, the ball is swept overboard. Noland jeopardizes his life swimming after it. But it drifts away, and is gone forever. Wilson is lost, but the castaway is saved. Clearly, Wilson functioned as a way for Noland to maintain human contact and conversation. We know it was an active dialogue because Wilson's answers appear in Noland's responses. In other words, not only did Noland preserve Wilson's half of the exchange but Wilson's evolving character—his difference, disagreements, and dissension—also supported the relationship.

The exchange was thus enervating. It did not just offer companionship; it offered the relationship of opposition. William Blake rightly maintained that "opposition is true friendship." It was an authentic voice because it did not obediently mirror one's own. Through that dialectic, it helped Noland not only to communicate but also to make critical decisions.

Can this personalized version of dialogue serve as a narrative metaphor for business and professional exchange? How familiar and beneficial is such dialogue especially to the process of those charged with making and communicating critical decisions? The linkage with communication is immediately apparent.

Dialogue, internal or external, not only mimics the communication process itself but also underscores the give-and-take of making decisions. One in fact can argue there are minimally three dialogues: one shapes the decision, another determines the communication of that decision to others, and the third dictates how to implement the decision.

We all know professionals who talk their way through their work. Sometimes it is internal, other times overt. In a number of cases, it also may take place in front of a client or colleague. "Let me see, you want to get this done, fast. Let me try this first; and if that does not work, I have a few other aces up my sleeve." If the customer is smart, he will sit quietly and listen to the oral problem-solving process as it makes its clever and circuitous way to a solution. The role of the listener is passive. He only has to pose the problem. He may have to answer a few questions along the way to refine and focus the problem, but that's all. He sits back and follows the dialogue, often finding it fascinating as he learns about the way this particular problem solver thinks and in fact solves problems. Although the solution obviously is the bottom line, observing the workings of a mind in a self-relationship process is equally absorbing and revealing.

Self-dialogue does not require another. Many people have conversations with their pets; some speak with favored inanimate objects or paintings or sculpture, which we may also touch. Some talk back to the radio or television. If viewers are really angry or annoyed, they express themselves by clicking it off or switching to another channel, usually accompanied by a few well-chosen exclamations. Others, contemplating but not yet deciding on a course of action, may initiate a dialogue in their heads and call in the warring opposites, one always stressing the downside, the other the upside—two different Wilsons, as it were.

The dialogue of self-relationship becomes a balancing act until enough accumulates to make a decision or to postpone it for another dialogue. Many CEOs and senior managers pay handsomely for this kind of dialogue in the form of executive coaches or trusted advisors.

Although it appears there is considerable value to the exchange, it is seldom acknowledged officially as a way of knowing. As a result, it is seldom taught, inculcated, and above all designed as a leadership or managerial tool. The structuring of dialectic self-relationships thus may improve problem solving, communication, decision-making, and even strategic planning.

Structuring a dialectic self-relationship minimally involves five process steps: scanning, selecting, formulating, trying out, and deciding. The five major stages are visually displayed in table 9.1.

Scanning

This first step is crucial. It involves an internal and an external inventory. For the dialogue and self-relationship to be effective, there must be self-candor. Thus, it is necessary to identify one's blind spots and the involvement of ego. True self-image, with all its blemishes and warts, must emerge if the dialogue is to stand a chance of being full and challenging.

A closed mind or defensive attitude will preclude flow and change. In short, receptivity has to be firmly established. It is balanced externally and objectively by the outcomes that are expected or the decision that has to be made. The bridge between the two worlds of dialogue and action prepares for and sustains the traffic across it.

Selecting

The screening process of preparing the objects of the dialogue, psyche and objectives, now sets up the selection of participants. A cast of characters has to be assembled. The first choice is to always ensure a

Table 9.1.   Process Steps of Dialectic Self-Relationship

Stages	Events/Behaviors	Outcomes
1. Scanning	Self-Inventory Goals	External/Internal Balancing
2. Selecting	Cast of Characters/Voices (Thesis/Antithesis)	360-Degree Inclusiveness
3. Formulating	Scene and Sequence	Reality Check
4. Trying Out	Evaluation	Revision
5. Deciding	Circular Conclusions	Priority of Alternatives

dialectic—minimally an advocate for one thesis, another for the antithesis. Others are selected to amplify the participants to create a miniature reality. For example, if certain managers and/or their divisions will be affected by the decision and how well it is communicated to them, a communications representative voice must be included.

If the central character has not had the best of experiences dealing with these other voices, he has to build into the process different versions of himself. He has to acquire an understudy who is enough like him for continuity but functions at another angle or frequency to test whether that alters the outcome of both the dialogue and the decision.

Formulating

It's time for an initial mock-up. For some it may take a visual form. Revealingly, the main participant may position himself in the middle. The dialogue may then take place all around him. Or he may distance himself from the entire exchange and lurk on the periphery. Whatever his location, the cast of characters is assembled and stages of discussion identified and sequenced.

A preliminary run-though is conducted to determine whether the cast of characters should be changed, added to, or subtracted from; and also at what point they should enter the fray. Anyone who plays chess and has to contemplate multiple moves is involved in strategic planning—estimating first, second, and third orders of impact, and understanding and feeling comfortable with such juggling. Once the number and kind of participants and the sequence are chosen, the dialogue is formally locked in and ready to proceed.

Trying Out

Like a play taken out of town for a tryout, all is set in motion in a limited way. Because the entire process is constantly circular, the focus here is evaluative. What has been left out? Is the major participant open enough or do we have to call in his understudy? Are the major participants representative of the whole? Have we left a key player out? Have the outcomes been stated directly and unequivocally? Do the representatives from other divisions properly embody or miniaturize the dynamics? Once revisions have been made according to a reality check, all is ready for the exchange to take place.

Deciding (Communicating and Implementing)

Whether or not a visual of the major players and their sequence has been made, it is probably helpful here not just to hear the voices, but to write down their talk in the form of a script. The dynamic of the exchange that way can then be reviewed. Such a recorded scenario also compels the major participant to get inside other characters and above all to express points of view other than his own. For the process to work its communicative magic, the voices all must be authentic.

The last task, before the curtain drops, is to record the solutions offered and the decisions made. If more than one, they need to be attributed to the different advocates and then prioritized. But they must all be saved, for they represent alternative solutions and decisions that still may be called upon or used as arguments to buttress the one selected. In addition, before one discards the entire process, like scaffolding after a building is complete, there may need to be one more use and distillation.

The key to the difference and distinction of the horizontal leader—his methodology—is his recognition and insistence that all decisions must be rendered as three decisions: the decision to do something, the decision as to how it will be communicated, and the decision on how it will be implemented. The dialogue must engage all three dimensions. Moreover, just as the decision-making process involved alternative options, so now the same process must be extended to accommodate the best ways to communicate and implement the decision.

Thus, the dialectic process is circular and bestows its configuration on the decision itself as well as its communication and implementation. Such dialogue also creates a check-and-balance system. If the decision made poses major problems of communication and/or of implementation, it must go back to the drawing board. The solution may be a problem. The gods of communication and implementation must be satisfied. If the decision fails its future tests of application, the dialogue must go back to square one.

A new decision or solution must be found that has to live and function in all the key dimensions of the real world and its cast of characters. Otherwise it will be stillborn or, worse, create problems bigger, tougher, and less repairable than the one that spawned the process in the first place.

It is this last gain that is particularly noteworthy and perhaps unexpected. The entire process seeks to bring about not only more effective decisions and solutions but also more effective leaders and managers. The new manager-leader is vivified, stretched, and extended by the dialectic of dialogue, and will be more inclusive, more balanced, more open, more diverse, and more multiple. In the final analysis the process is a form of professional development that is more holistic and dynamic than the traditional tunnel vision workshops on communication and decision-making skills.

We need to talk our way through to success. Listening and hearing voices may lead some to conclude that we are crazy, but crazy like a fox or a Plato.

Training Decision-Makers

Most communications training is after the fact. Once decisions have been made, new polices formulated, acquisitions and mergers agreed upon, then communications specialists are called in to wordsmith the announcements. Communications is never invited to play a direct and formative role in any of these processes; rather, it is involved only in their final formulations.

But often bad decisions are made, policies are inept, and mergers questionable. When that regrettably happens, the temptation is to return to the same process that created the problem in the first place, try to be more diligent next time, and expect a different outcome. But the problem may be endemic. It may involve the procedure itself or the range of participants or a conflictive interaction of both.

Converging process and personnel, it can be argued that communications might be a valued new partner to bridge the two. But for that to happen companies and trainers have to take the initiative and endow communications with more power as a contributing partner in critical business processes. For example, if chief learning officers (CLOs) trained decision-makers as to the muscular and proactive contributions communications can offer, there might be fewer lapses and failures. And if a rationale is needed to describe the benefits communications can deliver to decision-making, the following discussion may serve.

Communications minimally can bring three dimensions to current decision-making when invited as partner to the process at the outset. The first is to put the decision arrived at on pause in order to determine its "communicality." The second tests the capacity of various and often conflicting information sources to be sufficiently broad based, reconcilable, and integrated to elicit collective support. The third focuses on decision-making as a values process in which a series of smaller values decisions punctuates and stirs the final summative decision.

Proactive Role of Communications

In this instance, communication functions as a reality check. Managers can be taught the basics of anticipatory or proactive perceptions. How will this decision be perceived and received by a representative array of employees, customers, stakeholders, and shareholders? Is its "communicality" rating high or low? What are some of the ways it can be misunderstood or even distorted? To what extent is the decision a match or mismatch with the culture? Is it a fit with mission and expectations? Is it operationally savvy or is it a square peg being fitted into a round hole? Ultimately, will this decision affirm its makers or give the impression that the emperor has no clothes?

The responses to such questions of communications may be disturbing enough to put the decision on hold. Risk analysis thus becomes perceptions analysis. Communications thus functions as an advance guard, an anticipatory manager, and measurer of decision impact. Typically, decision-makers are too embedded and absorbed in the process to undertake 360-degree evaluation. They may be myopic and focused on the short term. But communications stands between the decision and those affected by it. Its allegiance is to those directly and indirectly impacted; it compels awareness of both immediate and long-term consequences. Managers are trained to see and walk both sides of the street. Communication simulates the voices of acceptance, rejection, or ambiguity. That feedback alone is sufficient to affirm or challenge the decision. In the latter instance it warns of failure or miscalculation. And its message then is clear: the decision in its present form and direction needs to be changed.

And with that powerful corrective, communication establishes its value as a special and perhaps equal partner in the decision-making process. In short, reconfigured and refocused through training, the decision process becomes a double process: the decision to do something and the decision to communicate that something.

Integrative Function of Communications

Communications also has the capacity to be a broker of information input into the decision process. Managers can be given workshops on data sources as alternate communication paths. The goal is always to identify the broadest base possible, on the one hand, and the durability and longevity of the life cycle of the data, on the other hand. To accomplish and converge that double focus, communications has to champion the integration of information over the long term. That future dimension tests the durability of the product or service, as well as its supporting information.

In the process, managers can appreciate the traditional persuasive power of communications as it seeks to coach various owners of information to share and to integrate sources and outcomes. Those putting forth trends, market segments, and customer buying profiles tend to be lone rangers riding their own hobby horses and pushing to be positioned as the number one source. Because communications alone embodies audience, it imparts the force of the collective to the decision-making process. It uniquely can serve as the gatekeeper and guardian of integrated data. If, as noted earlier, communications can serve to give voice to those impacted by decisions, here communications has to orchestrate a series of data soloists into a coordinated chorus. This is particularly critical because the common lament is that there is never enough data for decision-makers. What communications brings to that perennial gap is at least the optimization of available information.

Communications as Values Advocate

The competition of data is compounded by the competition of values. Teams bring forth value-laden recommendations, which even cross-functional teams, constituted as they are as a miniature of the whole, cannot harmonize. Assumed or implicit values driving data or recommendations are like the proverbial tip of the iceberg; the full extent is buried underneath. The missing role of arbiter can be legitimately assumed by managers using communications, in at least two points in the process, beginning and end.

Communications becomes an advocate of value trees analysis. Each team providing decision input has to make explicit the values driving their recommendations and, even more important, what trade-offs and alternatives can be offered to optimize broader corporate goals and mission value. Such vertical alignment can minimize unproductive conflicts. Moreover, alternatives offered can be used to negotiate upward final consensus.

But if the values process has been less than honest or total, communications may be called on to fill the values gaps. In particular, communications can stand at the receiving end and solicit values criteria for decision-making. Inevitably ranking or prioritizing will be required. Because communications is not directly involved nor does it favor any one recommendation over another, and because in effect its only allegiance is to optimizing the decision-making process, it can preside with equanimity. It enjoys the high road of the big picture, sometimes matching or even exceeding the range of senior staff, and thus when learned grants all managers executive perspective.

Hopefully at this point companies recognizing the value of communications training not only schedule such training, but also make it doubly inclusive. On the one hand, middle- and especially upper-level managers have to be persuaded to welcome communications into the decision-making process as a critical partner and ally at all levels. Minimally, in that capacity it can serve as an early warning system, practice damage control, help to establish a more integrated base for decision-making, and advocate an open values process so that decisions are in fact in alignment with company goals.

On the other hand, communications professionals themselves have to be prepared for the challenge of being differently and more comprehensively perceived and used. In particular, they have to learn to envision themselves as possessing unique skills and roles not provided by any other specialization. In other words, for the training to be effective, the trainers have to go outside the box and build into the workshops optimum interactive interfacing for both sets of participants.

Communications is the supreme middleman. It presides over the cracks between which data falls. It bridges and aligns the values gaps between competing team recommendations so that the final decision can be inclusive, diverse, transparent, and balanced. Above all, communications experts must directly and knowledgably enter the man-

Table 9.2. Contributions of Empowerment

Categories	Before Empowerment	After Empowerment
1. Structure	Centralized (Vertical)	Decentralized (Horizontal)
2. Job Description	Prescribed	Self-Directed
3. Mission Statement	Organizational	Employee
4. Operations	Function	Process
5. Employees	Workers	Assets
6. Leadership	Specified (Top-Down)	Distributed (Available)
7. Pay	Salary	Gains-Sharing
8. Human Resources	Recruitment	Retention
9. Relationships	Individual (Independence)	Group (Interdependence)
10. Training	Homogenous (Singular)	Heterogeneous (Cross-Divisional)
11. Information	Hoarded	Shared
12. Performance	Blame/Shame	Improvement
13. Manager	Boss	Coach
14. Listening	Limited/Selective	Feedback/Feed Forward
15. Decisions	Top-Down	Consensual
16. Innovation	R&D	Learning Organization
17. Forecasting	Planners	Lay Forecasting
18. Agreements	Contracts	Covenants
19. Voice	Singular	Multiple
20. Roles	Given	Negotiated

agement and operations fray. If they are to be brokers and advocates of vision and mission, and bring to the decision-making and operations process what is currently missing and what is uniquely theirs to provide, they must in fact act and perform like learning leaders. Indeed, communications so redefined may ultimately turn out be the best ally and extension of CEOs and senior staff.

Because communications takes place not only at the top but also at every decision point across the board, it miniaturizes and diffuses its connecting power and anticipatory function throughout the entire company at every level of decision-making and information gathering. Communications properly relearned, refocused, and championed can diffuse throughout the organization two contributions: the optimization of exchange—perhaps in itself the supreme mission of all trainers—and the advocacy of empowerment embodied in table 9.2.

But how all the above plays itself out in the emergence of compromise types is the focus of the next chapter.

The Emergence of Manager-Leaders   **10**

Double Transformation: Roles and Goals

MANAGERS AND LEADERS ARE CONSTANTLY juxtaposed. Most of the time it is a lopsided comparison not so much to honor the differences between the two but to preserve and elevate the distinctions of the latter. Table 10.1 shows a typical composite.

No wonder everyone wants to be leader and books on leadership far outnumber and outsell any on managers. In a typical three-ring circus of workers, managers, and leaders, the king of the hill always appears center stage. But aside from being a forced exercise of hype to make leaders look good at the expense of managers, there are a number of serious, pejorative, and perhaps unintended distortions.

The first is that the process of comparison and contrast fixes a rigid and myopic mind-set and lockstep upon managers, which may

Table 10.1. Composite of Managers and Leaders

	Managers	Leaders
Direction	Planning	Vision
Alignment	Controlling Boundaries	Creating Shared Cultures
Relationships	Focus on Objects	Focus on People
Role	Boss	Coach
Outcomes	Maintains Stability	Creates Change

ultimately be embarrassing to leaders. How are those limitations to be discarded, revised, or trained out of managers on their journey to the top? Evidently, it regularly fails because some CEOs are often criticized for behaving more like managers than visionaries or, worse, of being micro-managing leaders. But paralleling the two roles involves a more serious distortion: it obscures the current transformation of managerial roles.

Observation of the current actual behaviors of managers in diverse environments yields a profile that integrates rather than separates the two columns listed in table 10.1:

1. *Information Gathering.* Managers must scrutinize and maintain sources of organizational knowledge by developing information interfaces and internal networks.
2. *Market Competition.* Managers must observe, be knowledgeable about, and communicate the behaviors and reactions of competitive firms.
3. *Holistic Strategies.* The internal introduction of any major new system must be perceived and wired in place by managers. Their coordination is essential to managing the total impact on the entire organization and its decision-making process.
4. *Strategic Monitoring.* Because of fluid environments, managerial monitoring has become an important ally and adjunct of strategic planning. Aligned, both serve then as indicators not only of company direction but also of restructuring.
5. *Technology Supervision.* Every manager is now a technology manager whose task is to link and optimize information to achieve operational success.
6. *Consumer-centric.* Managers are responsible for creating, implementing, and aligning customer relationship management (CRM) systems and applications across divisions.
7. *Resource Optimization.* Managers oversee enterprise resource planning (ERP), which is a shared management tool used across the board to optimize both internal and external

resources accessible at an unlimited number of points to achieve higher levels of productivity.

8. *Financial Thread*. Managerial awareness of and contributions to financial and accounting processes are driven by cost control and cost savings.

9. *E-Commerce*. Managerial development and engineering of an e-commerce value chain is used to promote market adaptability and agility.

10. *Success Overlays*. Managers need to identify and communicate industry-level knowledge of critical success factors (CSF), especially those of innovation.

Although not all the above roles are assumed by all managers at any given time, it can be argued that some do even more. Given the historical and perhaps inevitable compulsion to glorify leaders and to minimize managers, a major corrective is in order. Indeed, most companies can operate (and often do) without leaders but would fall apart without the leadership of managers.

If the above list of additional functions is reviewed, what emerges is a new hybrid—the manager aggregated upward as a leader. The success of many companies in sustaining annual increases in productivity each year for the last fifteen has largely been brought about not by CEOs but by manager-leaders. But how did that happen? Three factors come into play: morphing goals, emerging roles, and thereby the general restructuring of the goals-roles of managers. All three exist in tandem and require a brief reexamination of the basic nature of the relationship between goals and roles.

Not all goals are morphing in nature. Traditionally, goals were stable, enumerated in job descriptions, and generally recognized as appropriate to the job title. Above all, they were familiar and accomplishable. Besides, if anything new surfaced, it was subsumed under the last line of "whatever it takes."

But then gradually and sometimes precipitously, some fixed managerial goals became more mercurial and even chameleon-like. They appeared to develop an elusive life and speed of their own. Workers and managers increasingly have become breathlessly involved in catching their own tail or constantly playing catch-up.

They also have become nervously accustomed to tasks being perennially incomplete and even out of reach.

But the remarkable achievement is that, even though all these new goals exceeded job descriptions, they somehow got done. And because such higher productivity was thankfully accomplished, even with downsizing, we generally failed to ask why.

It is an understandable sin of analytical omission. Targets were met, quality maintained, customers satisfied, market share retained, and so forth. The assumption was all would continue. All that was needed was to keep the pump primed and apply what had worked before: the pressure of competition and performance improvement training.

But the argument here is that the competitive demands will increase and that, if performance is to be maintained, there is a need to know the dynamics behind current success and reshape training accordingly. Specifically, learning and training have to be driven not solely by explicit and definable objectives but by goal-role reciprocity—by the dynamic interplay between task and talent.

Traditionally, the relationship between managerial goals and managerial roles was clear, static, explicit, and appropriate. Tasks were linked to roles and that was that. Spelling out such equivalents was in fact the function of job descriptions. But unknowingly stretching and changing goals compelled role changes. Managers had to shift into high gear, regularly exceed the parameters of their job descriptions, routinely embrace and implement new systems, and above all stir and train rank and file to function in teams and even become team leaders.

This unnoticed and pervasive series of transformations stemmed from the special, dynamic, and reciprocal relationship that secretly exists between morphing goals and changing roles. All stretch and mercurial goals carry within them the embryonic roles to accomplish those goals. The goals and roles are thus like secret sharers.

Conventional goals only require conventional managers. Morphing goals require manager-leaders. Managers had no other choice but to step up to the challenge, exceed their job parameters, and close the gap between emerging goals and moving targets—in short, to do whatever it takes.

The gulf between knowing and doing is being bridged by managers assuming roles previously reserved for those at the top. Managers have moved up the chain of command because of necessity not aggrandizement. The result is they now occupy and function across an enlarged and major center of the organizational chart.

In the process, hierarchy has essentially been leveled and given horizontal extent. The vision of distributed leadership has found its realization in the emergence of manager-leaders. But to be effective, traditional managerial training has to catch up and embody the dynamics and metrics of goal-role synergy. Thus what is now needed is training managers for their new leadership roles, rewriting their archaic job descriptions, and finally figuring out what to do with CEOs.

Although American workers are constantly on the stretch and routinely asked to do more with less, what is perhaps startling is that they have succeeded. Steady increases in productivity, profitability, and quality are being achieved even with downsizing. Why? Basically, there are two reasons: the sharp edge of global competition and performance improvement training. As far as the future is concerned, all that is evidently needed is more of the same: keep upping the ante and sustaining the learning. Right? Perhaps not.

There are two problems, one practical and the other conceptual. The workforce may encounter the law of diminishing returns. It may not be possible to continue to reach increasingly competitive goals especially with fewer employees and the thinning out of managers. In fact, the sign of a new substitution already has appeared: companies are outsourcing, especially abroad where wage differentials translate into immediate profitability. Actually the same cost-cutting ends are being achieved with in-sourcing. Circuit City replaced its entire commission-based sales force with fixed-pay employees at lower hourly wages. Others are following suit by replacing experienced and knowledgeable salespeople with clerks capable only of writing up orders. Customers have adjusted by becoming experts before entering the store.

Undoubtedly, more ingenious outsourcing and manipulative variations will surface as companies seek to remain viable and competitive. Financial experts and human resource professionals will attend conferences that display the latest cost-saving schemes. But still there may be limits to doing more with less. A quartet can be cut back to a trio, but it cannot perform a piece written for a quartet.

Can training pick up the slack and close the gap? Perhaps, but only through focused training that is more informed about those being trained. Thus, diagnostically driven training has surfaced—targeting training to hit the hot buttons of employees as revealed by extensive psychological and learning-styles testing. Such profiles certainly will bring greater precision and efficiency to reskilling. But valuable though such profiles are, they are essentially inward facing and partial. They tell more about workers but not about their work. And even when the two rightly are paired, the relationship between the two is often rendered in the static terms of column A as worker description and column B as work description.

A larger dynamic framework is needed whereby generic employee profiles can engage generic workforce patterns. Such interplay would recreate the reciprocal exchange between employee preferences and performance objectives. The framework being proposed here involves the transformation of the give-and-take relationship between work goals and roles.

Traditionally, goals are elaborate and roles simply stated. Goals are multiple, whereas roles are singular. Goals may alter or vary but the role remains the same. Moreover, goals and roles are not perceived as possessing a dynamic or changing relationship with each other. Rather, they are reassuring reflections of each other. Ideally, they are a mirror match.

A job title or role is linked with an appropriate set of goals, which in fact essentially defines that role. Thus, for example, performance evaluation is always set against goal achievement, not role change. In short, goals rule. That is where the action is. Because the focus is always on the action side of the equation, the role is regarded as static and given. It remains intact and the same.

That focus made sense especially in the past. Goals were manageable because they were of a piece with the given role and achievable because they did not stretch beyond the reach of that role. And even when such efforts routinely did exceed the parameters of both goals and role, no one noticed or cried foul because it was successful. There was no need to press inquiry further or employ closer scrutiny. Attaboys and congratulations were the order of the day as cheerleading managers expressed confidence in future replication. But it can be argued that what made such achievements possible was an unexamined and even undetected dynamic between goals and roles and that, when the nature of that secret interaction is known and tapped, it can yield a model for more targeted training and performance improvement, even upgrades.

The job classification process is both clarifying and imprisoning. It follows the paradox celebrated by Robert Frost's famous "Mending Walls": "Before I built a wall I'd ask to know/ What I was walling in or walling out." All jobs and job titles are also acts of positioning. They are sandwiched between one above and one below. The pyramid dictates the pecking order.

The detailed list of objectives that follows and accompanies each job title firmly establishes its role parameters. When spill-over occurs and is spotted as part of the evaluation process, it is often interpreted as a basis for a promotion or reassignment of greater responsibility. But only then is role change—usually a future one not the one under examination—contemplated as part of the process of goal achievement. In other words, all attention is fixed on goals, not roles, and hence on goal change, not role change.

But, as has been noted, times have changed. Not surprisingly, goals bear the imprint of such changes. Although they are no longer the same, the job description preserves them in amber and gives the illusion of continuity. But an overview and analysis of the workplace and the workforce reveals that goals have undergone at least five major generic transformations. They all have been stretched incrementally, even exponentially; targets have been altered while still in flight; alignment must be both vertical and horizontal; goals are constantly linked to structural and personnel cross-overs and cross-training; and the discontinuity of innovation must be embraced. A few words of explanation about each follow.

Stretch

Most current incremental increases are without end. They may even occur daily and often not evenly spaced. Except for their constancy they are not predictable in scope or degree. Like computer advances, they require constant updating and sometimes abrupt shifts brought about by paradigm changes. Constantly upping the ante, incremental stretch goals have become the new norm.

Moving Targets

Often even the incremental is not singular, but multiple; fan-like, not linear. Add-ons are the norm. Variations on threads are developed. Direction is altered. Updating and upgrading meetings are many and constant. There is little or no white space on the calendar. The pace is breathless. Heads-up regularly interrupts process. Evaluation occurs every Friday, sometimes daily, or tied to specific dates so as to capture the goals of the week. Flight plans or repairs have to be undertaken while en route. All must remain in motion. Everything is in a state of transition. Multitasking is now a generic task for all. Everyone has had to become a juggler.

Alignment

Individual and teamwork priorities are driven by alignment with divisional partners near and far and with company objectives. Organizational flow systems are nested within the larger big picture of vision and mission and serve as employee road maps of coincidence. But the priorities change, routinely and regularly. For large companies, the challenge is how to rapidly change the direction and momentum of an enormous battleship. Agility is what helped Jack be nimble and quick.

Cross-Overs

Structural reconfigurations into more open and fluid forms and functions increase and hasten cross-training and job rotation. In the process, even the lowest cog in the machine becomes many cogs. The overall shape of an organization comes to resemble more a series of rivers flowing through it than a tower of mechanical boxes. Accordingly, employee stretch goals become increasingly fluid, open-ended, and unfinished. Every job becomes a variation on a theme and every employee an artful dodger.

Innovation

Finally, all employees are asked to contemplate the discontinuity of job processes and functions. They are stirred to create alternative cost saving and more productive ways of doing more with less. Every aspect of the process has to become grist for the mill of innovation. The assumption is that everything, broken or not, needs to be fixed. Creativity is no longer the monopoly of R&D.

Although at any given time not all the above transformations may be operating at the same time, sooner or later they all will impact the workforce. They have to because they are driven by the unavoidable common force of competition that will not go away. To be sure, the above list may be so daunting and intimidating as to require moving the conventional last phase of all job descriptions— "And do whatever is necessary to accomplish the above"—to the first position. Such a generic catch-all would be somewhat redeeming when presented from the start. It would at least serve as a more accurate and appropriate warning of what has become increasingly undefined.

But the key obstacle to the application of this generic taxonomy is a mistaken focus on fixing or faulting only the fluid goals. When they are not met, the predictable explanation is that the objectives exceeded the parameters of the job description as well as the skills sets required to succeed. But when success occurs, we are so delighted that we give up being defensive but still fail to ask why and how.

So it is back to basics. Every goal houses the role that requires it to accomplish it. If they are not in synch, employees regularly complain and object to being unfairly judged. So they become territorial and defensive and complain, "That is not in my job description." Currently, that disparity is ignored by hard-pressed managers who respond with "Welcome to the new world." But what may be overlooked and lost sight of is a symptomatic mismatch. The kind of transformational-driven changes in goals that are required cannot be accomplished without role changes. Goals still may rule, but roles trump.

The argument here is that the current achievement of changing goals can only come about by changing roles. We have been so fixed on the goal side and its measurement and training that we have failed to recognize that a secret reciprocity exists between goals and roles. Certain goal changes cannot be accomplished without role changes.

Employees often unknowingly have to shift into high gear and alter behaviors and attitudes in order to reach their more demanding goals. But by failing to understand and value that new dynamic between goal and roles, managers and trainers have both failed to acknowledge the remarkable growth potential of employees and been ignorant of what is deeply at work in performance improvement and its evaluation.

To overcome those limits and to develop a more comprehensive and interactive basis for both training and assessment, two critical questions need to be answered: What kinds of goal changes require and even compel role changes? And what kinds of role changes emerge?

Clearly, not all goal changes stir role changes. Even some incremental ones may be different only in degree but not in kind. They thus still may be manageable and achievable and not require role change. But the five factors cited earlier do. The task now is one of dynamical linkages—to display (as in table 10.2) the matched goal-role relationships.

From these partnerships between goals and roles, two sets of conclusions may be drawn. The first describes the essential changing and reciprocal dynamics between goals and roles; the second redefines the new job descriptions driven by role performance upgrading.

Table 10.2.   Taxonomy of Goal-Role Exchanges

Morphing Goals	Role Changes
1. Incremental	Flexibility and Stretch
2. Multiple	Multitask and Entrepreneurial
3. Alignment	Priorities, Decisions, and Corrections
4. Variations	Open-Ended and Unfinished
5. Reconfiguration	Innovation and Implementation

Most current training focuses on goal transformations, not role changes. Most performance evaluations fail to factor in the changing relationships between morphing goals and morphing roles. Changing goals cannot be met without changing the roles required to achieve such objectives. Job descriptions create static expectations of a dynamic goal-role relationship and need to be totally redone. The ultimate and cumulative impact of goal-role metrics is the transformation of the workforce.

The correctives are clear. Training has to pair goals and roles and link emerging roles to reach morphing goals. Performance evaluation has to mirror and reinforce the training by measuring the emergence of roles appropriate to goal attainment. Job descriptions have to be brought in line by spelling out the unfinished nature of "whatever it takes" as the highest and ruling priority. Finally, learning and human resource directors have to contemplate that, given the transformation of performance goals, on the one hand, and the corresponding emergence of higher level roles, on the other hand, the upgrading required is more a matter of kind than of degree.

When the roles listed above are reviewed, what dramatically emerges is a new workforce definition of rank-and-file workers. Here then is the second set of conclusions. The roles compelled by morphing goals are essentially managerial in nature. Employees not only have to do but also manage their work. The level and kind of reflection and evaluation normally reserved for supervisors now is being exercised by those in the trenches. Monitoring, scheduling, and planning—traditional preserves of middle-level managers—now are routinely carried out by the rank and file.

Innovations of form and function are not lofty interventions introduced from above but created and accomplishable at the basic job level. New job descriptions have to be written for the emergence of the employee-manager. Goal-role changes have to become the new and future focus of training and evaluation. But their application has to be revised so as to develop not employees but employees as managers.

Such a dramatic change at the base reverberates throughout the entire organization and not only alters but also parallels the new goal-role changes of managers and leaders. Collectively, they constitute the emerging workforce of the future.

Patchwork Leaders and Alphabet Soup **11**

TYPICALLY AND EVEN TRADITIONALLY, discussions of the future of leadership in general and of CEOs in particular stress the need for new visions and goals. Although what that shall include may vary significantly with different organizational and sector priorities and urgencies, it will undoubtedly include globality, forecasting, information networks, learning management systems, and, most important, the pressure to integrate all of the above.

But if such projections portend a substantial and even radical change in CEOs, should not who they are, where they are coming from, and where they will be heading be as important as what they will have to do? Should not new goals be linked to new roles? Perhaps in the process even the familiar executive acronym may be altered. Indeed, here are at least five new titles for CEO drawn from the alphabet soup of the future:

CIO
CLO
GBO
CIC/CIA
CIP

Whether or not any of these prevail over time or appear officially on the masthead, they do serve to identify and perhaps to define the new dynamics of top leaders and why the new focus on recasting goals and visions surfaced in the first place. Above all, they may demonstrate that the CEO of the future, like the organization he leads, will not be a singular but a multiple composite, not a lone ranger but a hybrid blend of diverse associates. In any case, exploring and examining each new pretender to the throne may tell us more about the seat of power than what only the current discussion of new goals has yielded so far.

CIO as CEO

This top-level position of chief information officer (CIO) is the creation of information technology and systems. In some organizations the CIO is designated as chief of information technology (CIT) to signal and symbolize the degree to which all business has become e-business. Indeed, all courses in current MBA programs are officially or unofficially e-courses to dramatize the extent to which research and information sources are web based. In some instances the Internet serves as the only current library available.

The CIO is responsible for creating, maintaining, and structuring organizational data and information flow. The extent to which that is increasingly the life blood and circulation system of companies has determined the elevation of the director of IT to CIO. What also has pushed that position forward to the executive level and even to the point of becoming the CEO is the addition of data decisions. Embedding just-in-time and real-time data in all internal and external operations has brought new transparency and precision to decision-making, the key task of top-level executives.

CLO as CEO

The chief learning officer (CLO), whatever his initial specialization, is a generalist. His discipline and expertise is generic learning. He creates, manages, and evaluates learning management systems that operate vertically from top to bottom and horizontally across all divisional lines and provide e-training 24/7/365.

The CLO is the heir apparent to Peter Senge's learning organization. His immediate and ongoing principal task is to increase productivity, profitability, quality, customer satisfaction, and market share-margins through knowledge acquisition and management. His long-term goal is to help create and train the workforce of the future. That visionary prospect alone qualifies the CLO to be a CEO.

What also reinforces that equivalency is cost-control driven assessment. CLOs constantly evaluate offerings to determine whether they in fact are implemented by all, across the board, and bring about the desired degree of performance improvement. CLOs are ruled by return on investment (ROI), as are all CEOs.

GBO as CEO

The global business officer (GBO) is an empire-building executive who operates in two ways and directions simultaneously. First, he creates a miniature of the whole. Depending on existing structures, it either serves as a global overlay for all operations and levels or subsumes them all under a new international imperative. Second, a GBO dramatizes the extent to which companies envision themselves and their future to be global in nature, scope, and focus. When all three combine and become the primary goal, the GBO may become the CEO.

But even as an intermediate position, the GBO is mission critical. He offers a center that is often lacking altogether or only occasional and partial: a global mind-set. The task of the GBO is to facilitate the diffusion of that new ideology throughout the entire organization and to spell out the opportunities and challenges of global markets and customers. As overseas numbers climb and reach the point of matching or exceeding national sales or when profit margins are greater than those of domestic operations, the prospect of a GBO becoming CEO will proportionately increase.

CIC/CIA

Progress is always incremental but it is not often holistic as well. Intellectual capital (IC) or intellectual assets (IA) qualifies on both counts. IC was developed initially by Skandia to bring more realistic criteria and greater precision and detail to the evaluation of company assets. Book value and annual reports not only failed to reflect critical but often intangible assets, but also in the process distorted both market capitalization investment and stock purchases. The correctives involved required a total conceptual overhaul, not just tweaking the financials. That involved factoring in both tangible and intangible assets like human capital and R&D until all the parts summed up a new whole. As IC became the shaping structure of organizations, it seemed a natural progression for a CIC or CIA to become a CEO.

CIP

This title may appear initially mischievous but what is behind it is instructive. Jacob Jaskov claims to be the first chief innovation pusher (CIP). Not accidentally, Jaskov is a futurist and active member of the Copenhagen Institute of Futures Studies. Indeed, he even suggests that his role is totally future driven.

The essential thrust of his new title is innovation. Minimally, creativity will be so critical to future success that it is future creating. The CIP thus will preside over a future time that will be so constantly and intensely new that as much as 90 percent of everything may appear different. Reinforcing and accelerating that prospect will be the singularity that is projected to produce more progress in the first two decades of the twenty-first century than in all previous periods combined. Future shock may have to be redefined as future displacement. Past inventory will be replaced by future cornucopia. Innovation will be the front and back of change and may even become its synonym. The company that redefines change as innovation will, according to Jaskov, inherit the future and ultimately replace its CEO with a CIP.

In summary, table 11.1 exhibits the major CEO alternatives.

There remains one final matter to discuss. How will all or any of this come about? Are current CEOs less egocentric than those in the past and therefore more accepting of leadership-sharing? Have they been differently educated or trained to recognize and be receptive to these new executive-level trends and usurpations?

When was the last time a training program for CEOs was offered? Evidently, everyone else needs it, but CEOs are finished learning or

Table 11.1. Alternatives to CEOs

Title	Shaped/Driven By	Future Goals and Gains
CIP	Information Technology	Data-Decision Systems
CLO	Knowledge Acquisition	Future Workforce
GBA	Global Competition	Worldwide Operating Systems
CIP/CIA	Other than Financial Assets	New Integrated Enterprises

else that task has been turned over to a private or invisible executive coach or trusted advisor. In other words, aside from the shock of the new and its future-driven executive titles, the comfort zone of most current CEOs would preclude wholesale adoption.

Thus once again gradualism rules the day. At least three less dramatic and more gradual courses of action surface. The first involves the CEO as hybrid; the second an amplified CEO executive team; and the third a two-tiered executive layer, one traditional and the other transitional.

CEO Hybrid

The CEO may in fact have come from one of the key new areas, or the changing direction of his company may have compelled his becoming a quick study. He also may be a she and not American-born or both, and thus more reflective of the demographic and market shifts of the company. In any case, current CEOs have the option to choose a new partner identity, and to exist as a hybrid before circumstances force such collaboration.

Executive Team Reconstituted

If the CEO prefers remaining intact, he may shift the need for change from himself to his executive team. Typically, that minimally consists of a COO and CFO and sometimes also the head of HR and the head of legal. The latter may have been elevated to that level because of mergers and acquisitions. To that inner circle, all five or a selection of the above could be added. It may not be an easy fit. The new team members may be younger, culturally more diverse, speak in technical terms or different paradigms, and behave like young and impatient Turks storming the barricades. It is thus not unlike putting two very different families together and, the Brady Bunch notwithstanding, it is no easy or successful task.

The CEO may have to become involved in conflict reduction and resolution. He may have to calm the waters, as well as exploit and direct the tensions toward shake-up. But sooner or later he must forge a new diverse executive team with members who are all on the same page. That may require a retreat. With this polymorphous group, it may require one every three months.

Two-Tiered System

The prospect of such interpersonal turbulence, as well as the jockeying for power and leverage, may lead the CEO to pause. If the traditional and older members have his ear they may heighten uncertainty. They may argue that these new titles and areas of expertise are unproven flashes in the pan or advanced by and for obvious self-interest and self-promotion. They may ultimately suggest that these new areas can be subsumed under traditional operations and thus the company need not incur the additional expenses of a new executive-level appointment as well as their expensive staff. But if the CEO has any vision at all, he will hearken to the directions of the future.

The CEO will move toward compromise. He will create a two-tiered executive team. One will be traditional and the other transitional. Like the choices of column A and column B, they can exist in different combinations.

The CEO has a number of options. He can make them equal, meet with them separately, and combine them for certain topics such as long-range planning. Or he can elevate one team over the other, permanently or temporarily. He even may set them at odds with one another by assigning both the same task.

But whatever variations on the theme of future leadership are played, the position of CEO itself is now beset by the same forces of change buffeting his organization. Indeed, the first order of business may be to set the executive house in order as the threshold for developing company-wide future plans. The challenge now is that there are many new and eager firsts.

Not the least is mastering what is next—transition.

Leaders and Transition **12**

ALL TRAINING FOLLOWS THE SAME paradoxical rhythm. It combines reassurance with change and affirmation of the status quo with incremental advances. In short, it straddles present and future. It is thus inevitably persuasive, coaxing the now and the given to include more—and more that is different—beyond its original benchmark position.

But such venturing forth from one's comfort zones typically is eased by offering only modest and digestible bites and bytes. However, the pressing issue now is change management. Indeed, the need for that larger competence has led to questioning whether incremental gains are comprehensive and sufficient enough to play catch up, let alone to be ahead of the game. Then, too, the expectation is that engaging and mastering discontinuity also may bring the workforce closer to the threshold of creativity.

But as in all training the bold needs to be anchored in the familiar. So the search initially is always for what is in-house—already existing examples of change management and creativity—as well as what affects the entire workforce. In other words, what stimulates creativity should be sufficiently mainstream so that if innovation does not occur, there is still the consolation of mastery.

Who then are the most innovative types? Invariably, three groups appear. The first are the entrepreneurs. These perpetual motion and restless start-up protean types live on the edge of change. Their career path is measured not so much by how many jobs they have had but how many businesses they have created. They generate unlimited variations on a theme, exhibit spin-off thinking, and often display the uncanny ability of being ahead of the pack. Or as Wayne Gretzky claimed, "I skate to where the puck is going to be, not where it has been." They are a marvel and often exhausting to be around.

The second group is comprised of those managerial coaches whose stock and trade are challenging workers to change. Their value resides in their ability to read signs, decipher the handwriting on the wall, and operate as early warning and opportunity agents to those they mentor. Their success is always reciprocal.

Finally, there are all the exceptional professionals and project managers found in all organizations and all sectors who are routinely transformational and transactional. They are endless advocates of training and unlearning, finding collaborative ways of doing things differently, and leapfrogging: "While we are catching up, let us also get ahead."

What characteristics do all of the above have in common?

- Living and thinking ahead of their time.
- Impatient with and even disdainful of current paradigms.
- Always negotiating change—one state to another.
- Keen sense of the dynamics of implementation—reality checks of scenario and simulation.
- Imagining and creating what did not exist before.
- Inclusive, integrative, and collaborative.
- Patchwork cobbling—always putting together holistically what is separate.
- Thriving on and managing risk and blur.

What stirs such innovative types? Are there special contexts, conditions, and cultures that are not only a match but a spur for their creativity? If one steps back and observes their performance, what dynamics emerge as norms?

- Their goals always are moving targets.
- Performance evaluations correspondingly have to occur more often, sometimes daily.

- Mid-course corrections are regular adjustments.
- Job descriptions are regularly exceeded and outdated.
- Cross-over operations and integration are routine.
- Nothing and no one remains intact.

Such workforce impacts are so far beyond the norm that even the standard and familiar answer of change addresses only symptoms not causes, business-as-usual practices not basic assumptions. Perhaps what is needed is a deeper definition of change—one that engages not just branch but also root, and above all directly reflects the new everyday working reality of employees.

The standard expectation is that when dislocation or disruption occurs, it will be both temporary and non-recurrent. It is a singular event that happens every once in awhile but, if we are just patient and stoical enough, everything will return to the way it was. After all, cycles of ups and downs are familiar and inevitable. But suppose a transition lasts a very long time, much longer than previous transitions? Or worse, suppose that the transition finally gives way not to reassuring and familiar stability but to another transition? And further that that transition is then replaced by another and still another, and so on and so on? What then?

When that happens often enough and lasts long enough then transition, not stability, becomes the norm; then we confront the paradox of continuous discontinuity. The only problem is that we have not been trained to recognize, let alone accept and engage, transition as a permanent and recurrent reality. Instead, we worship the absolute god of stability.

But what if instead one were to acquire another outlook entirely? Perceive transition as not the exception but the rule? With such expectations, we would not have to develop surprise-free forecasts. Surprise would rise every day with the sun. Rather than avoiding change or running away from threats of novelty, they would be a daily occurrence. It might even be welcomed as a new constant and not an occasional variable. Above all, transition would normalize continuous improvement as the minimum response of keeping up. It also would optimally stir innovation to be the new version of incremental gains.

There is a need to provide transition training for the entire work-force. But how? Three immediate directions surface. First, consideration should be given to creating special and separate workshops on transition as a common orientation for all new hires at all levels. It would extend the typical discussion of company values to include company operating assumptions. The conventional statement of "This is how we do things around here" has to be supplemented with "This is why we have to do those things this way." Performance expectations thus would be embedded in the metrics of the company's operational reality.

Second, mission and vision statements should be reviewed to determine to what extent if at all they embody the norm of transition and the performance expectations associated with workforce reality. Third, employing transition as an overlay not an overhaul, all training offerings should be reviewed to determine to what extent they support both the continuous and disruptive nature of transition. Where lacking, a healthy dose of the temporary may have to be injected. All offerings thus would embody the new principle that all performance is a work in progress. There are no longer any final goals. The endgame has become the ongoing game.

Persuading employees to embrace transition as a permanent condition of daily work may be eased by developing and offering a taxonomy of transition in the form of a performance template. Although additions and supplements can be encouraged, the information in table 12.1 perhaps can serve as common ground.

Trust is based on truth. In this instance, it requires telling the truth about the new reality of work. That in turn needs to be fol-

Table 12.1. Taxonomy of Transition

	Past	Present	Future
Goals	Given	Stretch	Embryonic
Evaluation	Annual	Multiple	Daily
Tasks	Singular	Multitasking	Crossover
Focus	Divisional	Team	Interoperable
Structure	Vertical	Horizontal	Intersecting
Leadership	Hierarchical	Shared	Diffused
Innovation	Limited	Accessible	Required

lowed by the various ways new performance expectations and evaluation metrics are being shaped and driven by the new norm of transition. Far from shrinking from the challenge, the workforce not only may welcome the truth of what is in fact their familiar daily reality but also bring new mastery and creativity to the reality of permanent change.

Or sometimes not—see the next chapter.

Leaders and Endgames **13**

THINKING AHEAD IS GENERALLY not something many professionals or companies do easily, regularly, or systematically. Indeed, lest it not be done at all or poorly, the task is typically assigned to special groups: strategic planners, new product teams, and market demographers. In addition, the expectation is that overall vision, which is the unique preserve and perspective of top leadership, will provide the steerage of survival and growth. That is usually as far as it goes; in the past that was sufficient. But now a new imagination has been stirred and let loose.

The future has become busier, more restlessly new, and more intrusive. A new more anticipatory frame of mind is increasingly being stirred into being. It is alternatively creative and paralyzing, uplifting and despairing, open to and closed off from the future. It is affecting both job and lifestyle expectations and thus inevitably shaping the morale and productivity of both the workforce and the general citizenry. In short, it cannot be ignored.

To comprehend the scope and depth of imagining both the dark and the bright side of the future requires investing disconnects with the power of divergent thinking. And nothing stirs normal paranoia like encountering the ends of things—events and processes being illuminated and triggered by a series of what could be called endgames. Although regrettably there are many such endgames that often appear with in-your-face persistence, at least three are illustrative of the 360-degree convergent impact of having to imagine the unmanageable.

Work Endgame

Jobs are no longer secure. An estimated 3.3 million service jobs will move out of the United States in the next ten to fifteen years. Between downsizing and outsourcing, and the decline of the manufacturing and now the service sectors, the workplace has become for many not only an uncertain and precarious place but also a fertile breeding ground of cynicism.

If fear of job and income loss becomes the dominant motivator, what impact does such a frame of mind have on training and leadership? Will executive encouragement be cynically viewed as merely a manipulative way of extending productivity before the inevitable ax will fall? Why wait? Why not bail out as soon as possible?

American Endgame

The United States is being used. It is not only the place where jobs leave. It also may become the place where American professionals also leave. For the first time in its history, the United States may see a significant portion of its population emigrate due to superior overseas opportunities. Acceding to forecasts, Generation Y, the segment born between 1978 and 1995, may be the first US generation to spend large portions of their professional lives, if not all their adult lives, overseas.

Planet Earth Endgame

As if that were not enough, planet vulnerability has become a frequent endgame. The prospect of global warming has invested coastlines with real urgency. The enormous populations of China and India and their pursuit of the American dream of consumption have given new and terrible meaning to global competition and environmental impact.

In short, there is now a new competition for the imagination. Can it be stirred and directed toward innovation or will it be consumed by apocalypse? For better or worse, vision and mission—the mainstays of leadership—have become now the workforce battleground. The wake-up call for CEOs is to sustain an innovative America.

But how? By reviving a faculty often rarely invoked and by granting it central status as antidote to endgames—the imagination.

Typically and understandably, training is after-the-fact. It functions as a midwife—between the conventional and the current. It regularly is involved in catching up, updating, and recalibrating. Although not new itself, its recurrent task is to equip the workforce with the current state of the art. Thus training is more object than subject, more a follower than a leader.

The argument here however is that, if CLOs are truly leaders, that arrangement has to change. Training has to be both at and beyond the cutting edge—not solely reactive but also anticipatory. In short, training should obediently follow paradigm shifts along with discovering and advocating for such total repositioning. Training should not solely implement R&D; it should also create its own research. Two recent dramatic examples may serve to document the case.

The Center for Resource Economics in Washington, DC, recently launched a new publishing venture, Island Press, which specializes in global environmental issues as they impact nation-states and multinational corporations. Although the series displays the characteristic and familiar documentation and depth of solid scholarship, there are at least two dramatic differences that set these works apart and may carry implications for training.

First, interdisciplinarity is a norm. To be sure, many of the works are multiply authored and thus nicely approximate the whole by parceling out the range of interoperability to a team. But quite a few are individually written and yet sustain that same scope. The net result is the impression of a new breed of professionals producing studies and engaged in problem solving distinguished by routinely employing cross-over specializations. In short, global range is matched by disciplinary range to the point where the two not only sustain but also enrich each other.

The second pattern is perhaps more surprising. Again and again in the midst of intense analysis, data displays, and geopolitical systems, there is the unexpected call upon the imagination. Thus, one work seeks "to produce controversy and stir the imagination." Another couples "resilience thinking with creative and imaginative thinking." Still another addresses biogeochemical cycles and calls for both a scientific and imaginative reassessment of interdependence. Such coupling of analysis and imagination may also suggest that interdisciplinary study now requires contexts sustainable only by imaginative constructs.

In any case, typically, neither subject is currently part of most training menus. The closest would be facilitating team difference but that seldom involves different disciplines. Workshops on innovation may approximate the emphasis on imagination, but the term is seldom, if ever, used or invoked, probably because it is too fanciful or precious.

Clearly, given current training preferences and priorities, adoption is not likely to occur at least without an urgent and compelling rationale. What kind of rationale would be required for CLOs to become advocates of the above two training shifts? And what would be their key leverage points? Generically there are always five:

1. New training reinforces, energizes, and extends all current workforce improvement efforts.
2. It is next-generation problem solving and thus offers innovative competitive advantage.
3. It will attract and retain cutting-edge talent.
4. No one else is doing it.
5. It is doable, hopefully within budget.

But even if that opens the door, advocacy also requires specificity to carry the day. Why interdisciplinarity and why should training do it? Because convergence and cross-overs increasingly rule productivity and profitability. The problems of today and tomorrow require synthesis of integrated concepts and mastery of multiple disciplines.

All current in-house specialists operate within the box of singular perspectives and are stuck in the repetitive success of past tool kits. The topic cannot be subcontracted out because it is not currently an integral part of most academic programs. Most important, a crash course can begin to produce interdisciplinary cross-overs in six months. And follow-up evaluation can tap existing monitoring of team performance and even allow for team leaders to customize further development to optimize team range.

But arguing for imagination is not that easy or direct. Instead, it calls for more space—more rethinking, more stepping back, and setting up different sets of expectations and modes of expression. Although examples abound, we may be reluctant to use them. Sadly, our current imagination is more preoccupied with terminus than genesis, the horrific rather than the hopeful.

Increasingly, we are being lead by global warming and nuclear rogue nations to think about the unthinkable and to imagine the unimaginable. That often leads to being overwhelmed and the despair of imagining the unmanageable.

On a more mundane and personal level, but in the final analysis equally devastating and reinforcing, we witness companies and industries end and even our own jobs vanish or disappear abroad. In other words, it is not as if the contemporary imagination is absent or irrelevant. Unfortunately, it is very much with us but in terrible forms. So the first step is to recognize that, although the contemporary imagination now inhabits the dark side, it does not have to remain there. Indeed, one of the supplementary gains of training would be to strike and even restore balance.

But how? By starting with where and what we are. We have to recognize that the modern imagination is more comfortable inhabiting the world of science fiction than that of business-as-usual. Scenario is its preferred form of communication. The creating of multiple worlds is in fact its favored form of analysis.

In short, the starting point of training is normalizing the assumptions of science fiction and the discipline of scenario construction. But lest such encouragement and development of such divergent thinking go too far afield, applications can be paired. The basic laws of the science faction imagination can be brought to bear upon and redefine the often unacknowledged operating assumptions of modern businesses challenges. The following are three laws of the science-fiction imagination.

Vulnerability
The obsessive question of the imagination is "What if?" Its focus is to compile and tally risks; its object of inquiry is always systemic. Overall continuity is not assured. The search is for the weakest links; for review of recent decisions that increased vulnerability no matter the trade-off benefits; and for company change that exacted a future price. It is often the little things that can undo you. The micro can disturb the macro; the law of crash is slip.

Excesses
Hubris is failing to respect limits: the carrying capacity of operating systems, the reliability of what is not adequately maintained, performance expectations in excess of skill sets and training updates. All excesses are ultimately cumulative and approach the law of diminishing returns.

Myopia
Not anticipating the unintended consequences of actions, subjecting vision constantly to subservience to mission, adding one more sheep to the already compromised commons—all these are rehearsals for demise and all rest on the assumption of endless growth and consumption. But a law of escalation is at work in science fiction.

The future is offered in three forms: stretch, strain, and shock. Not looking ahead combined with decision paralysis surrenders options. What was initially reasonable but forsaken (stretch) gives way to the grim (strain) and finally to the draconian (shock).

The imagination of science fiction is thus always an endgame. Indeed, it often begins with terminus and then in brooding fashion takes us back to genesis—to where we went wrong. But what we fail to appreciate is the extent to which the apocalyptic imagination is also analytical, and further because its scope is total and inclusive it is finally also interdisciplinary. In the process, history never totally abandons us. It puts in our hands the means to comprehend the future of the future and hopefully this time to arrive at a new leadership point—where sustaining replaces controlling, where managing replaces dominating, and where vulnerability, excess, and myopia properly addressed can transform science fiction into its historical twin of the utopian imagination. And such transformations are always the goals of innovative leaders. Sometimes, as noted in the next chapter, it requires the extraordinary act of creating cultures.

Leaders as Creators of Cultures **14**

Leaders of innovation specialize: they either model it like Thomas Edison, Steve Jobs, and Bill Gates or they create innovation cultures like 3M or GE. They seldom do both. The latter is harder, not so much because there are no models to emulate but rather because emulation is not the right way to go; it leads to improvements that are passed off as innovation. Inspiring slogans on training walls are equally prematurely satisfying.

In other words, the major obstacle is substitution: settling for the incremental or the visioning. Where do these limited definitions and expectations come from? In most cases, from company training.

The current learning agenda of organizations is formidable. Minimally, three issues are pressing. First, how do we replace productivity with innovation as the new source of competitive advantage? Indeed, the current preoccupation of finding ways to stir creativity has become so obsessive that it is almost herd-like. But if we all move collectively to think outside of the box, have we only succeeded in carrying the box with us?

Second, learning program array is primarily preoccupied with updates and upgrades—with small and manageable incremental and sequential improvements—and not with complete changes of direction. So we are locked in by what we do well.

Finally, the ante has been upped. The prod is not just change but discontinuity—managing and surviving the enormous gaps between labor and machines, outsourcing and employment, domestic insularity and global traffic, organizational charts and informal networks, face-to-face and virtual teams, free trade and treaty capitalism.

Although the list of gaps and disconnects is serious and almost endless, the focus on innovation tends to be small and narrow, almost frivolous and self-centered, and floats free of any of the big issues that in fact have made it necessary in the first place. It is thus without context, without cause and effect, without history.

But why should it be so burdened? Because innovation is essentially a futures exercise. It not only constitutes the history of the future but also marks its creation—and as such grants companies so driven new life and longevity.

But isn't that a little heady—a bit big to take on? Typically we are better at fixing, tinkering, or tweaking than replacing—avoiding at all costs creating a totally new culture even though the handwriting to do so is on the wall. And so typically we settle on what is doable and deliverable—on piecemeal or smaller versions of all the major challenges so that they can be made more manageable as singular and unconnected, definable and researchable, clear and ambiguous issues.

But in the process we have ignored the telltale intrusions of a totally new and 360-degree future. We know intuitively and statistically that we will have to live in a brave new world but we are not sure how to get there, who will lead the charge, and what it will look like when we arrive—above all, how to start. Happily, there are five steps to begin with.

Leadership

Culture change is a CEO focus. Leadership is affirmed and confirmed when two factors converge: when what has to be done can be done only by top leadership and when what is required can come only from a singular and urgent initiative of executive vision. That in turn may define what companies should search for in a new CEO or, better still, become the expectation of the current holder of the office, whose change would dramatize the organizational capacity to pursue a totally new direction. In either case, CEO and the future have to become one.

Start Small But Everywhere

Assemble, review, and adjust ever so slightly and slyly all in-house frameworks and timetables. Enlarge parameters to include more than before—approximate gradually 360 degrees. Encourage not stopping short at the present or even the short term but pushing, no matter how tentatively, a little further—acting like an advanced guard—and then reporting back what is found out and aggregating such feed-forward-feedback upward to strategic planning as an early warning/ opportunity system.

Also gather together a team of vice presidents and ask them to look carefully at all the ongoing processes they supervise and see whether any can accommodate a more look-ahead perspective. For example, can performance evaluation include a speculative component and anticipate what changes might impact each job and its future performance? See how many across-the-board little leaps ahead can be quietly built-in and wired in place.

Not Alone

Signal that you are not the only ones involved in this journey into uncharted waters—that you have colleagues, even partners. Create a futures page on your website (along with room for blogging) that lists the World Futures Society (which celebrated its seventy-fifth anniversary in 2008), its global counterparts in Copenhagen and Rome, the 3000 year project, climate change organizations, and so forth.

In other words, establish credibility and link your culture change to what is being supported and undertaken by many respected professionals and organizations in what is gradually taking on the dimension of a collective and worldwide movement. Send some of your vice presidents and senior managers to attend different annual futures conferences. Meet with each afterwards for breakfast, note any changes in language, and listen for any newness; excitement would be a bonus.

How Will You Know When You Get There?

There are two ways you will know you are *there*. First, conversations will change. There will be a little more buzz and electricity in the air. Exchanges will be more frequent, entangling, breathless, and hurried; the focus will be different, lighter, more curious, and even philosophical. There will also be a bit more playfulness and mischief: "What if" will replace "Yes, but." Ideas will be put forth and introduced with a new apology: "This may sound crazy but suppose . . ." Above all, there will be more enthusiasm and excitement. Exclamation points will return to emails, and conversations will resemble those of a start-up.

Second, proposals to do things differently will begin to appear—from all areas and divisions—and range from the incremental to the innovative, from small to big, from the continuous to the discontinuous, from new, better, and shorter ways of doing things to total breakthroughs. (Remember, after all, that if you eliminate a step in a theorem that is then known as an elegant proof.) All need to be equally welcomed and valued. The eureka moments should not crowd out everyday improvements, which grant daily and incremental competitive advantage. Occasionally, a blockbuster will surface. Inevitably it will take on the form of a new business, one that never existed before and that is revolutionary. If seized, it will grant your company a new lease on life. If ignored, it may be taken up by your competitor and put you out of business. Executive vision thus may start it all, but executive initiative still must be there to act and to save the day and convert the future into the present.

Turn the Future Over to the Workforce

Not trickle down but bottom up, not vertical but horizontal, not along divisional but cross-divisional lines—shake-up and engage all personnel at all levels with the future of their jobs and the company. It can't be otherwise if the objective is changing an entire culture and for invention to become the new norm and everyday expectation. The CEO's goals? To become the future, to give it voice and vision, to bring all together as creative partners.

Finally, what it would take for conventional company cultures to become innovative ones? Table 14.1 proposes such development.

Although the forms innovation may take are perhaps infinite, what is clear is that organizations can stir, stimulate, and structure its

Table 14.1. **Summary of the Culture Conversion Factors**

Subject Area	Conventional Cultures	Innovative Cultures
Information	Impeding	Facilitating
Focus	Branch	Root
Structure	Pyramidal	Disaggregated
Leadership	Concentrated	Diffused
Work Profiles	Defined	Evolving
Knowledge	Familiar	Discovered
Resources	Outsiders	Insiders
Productivity	Incremental	Out of the Box
Team Range	Divisional	Interoperable
Team Management	Directed	Benign Abandonment
Empowerment	Partial	Total
Evaluation	Blaming	No Fault
Training	Updating	Futurizing

emergence. As table 14.1 indicates, the options and approaches are many and reinforcing.

The value of focusing on the centrality of the workforce is that it takes an organization to its operational core. It exposes its basic inquiry modes, information structures, problem-solving and decision-making processes, and performance expectations and measures. Such anatomical analysis of basic assumptions inevitably involves identifying work profiles for review and revision. The net result is the development of alternative work profiles. When implemented through refocused training and recruitment, a new workforce driven by research, information totality, and team forensics begins to emerge and leave its collective mark on company culture.

No partnership can match that between innovation and the workforce to provide the pervasive leverage and capacity to shape company culture into an agent of innovation. In this instance the chicken-egg problem contains its own happy solution. But what remains unresolved is finding unity in flux.

THE DYNAMICS OF
FIVE LEADERSHIP TYPES

III

The Profile of the Transformational Leader

THE CHANGER

MUCH OF THE DIFFERENCE AND DISTINCTION of transformational leaders is that they are often unpredictable. They go against the grain; they forsake the conventional wisdom. They are artful dodgers; they are big-stake players and gamblers. To appreciate the range of such independent thought and action, here are a number of examples.

Mea Culpa

To the surprise of many, GM unexpectedly issued a public apology and confessed its many sins recently in a full-page ad in *Automotive News* magazine:

> While we're still the U.S. sales leader, we acknowledge we have disappointed you. At times we violated your trust by letting our quality fall below industry standards and our designs become lackluster. We proliferated our brands and dealer network to the point where we lost adequate focus on our core U.S. market. We also biased our product mix toward pickup trucks and SUVs. And we made commitments to compensation plans that have proven to be unsustainable in today's globally competitive industry. We have paid dearly for these decisions, learned from them and are working hard to correct them by restructuring our U.S. business to be viable for the long-term.

Whether or not all CEOs should go public, tough times invite—some would argue compel—honest and unflinching reflection on questionable and failed policies, practices, and procedures. No company or leader is faultless. Purgation at least sets the record straight.

Repositioning

Although confession helps wipe the internal slate clean, it is not analysis. It does not address why and what—the drivers of doom—causes the perfect economic storm. The CEO thus has three choices: to acknowledge, manage, or explain the hard times. Clearly all are necessary, although the weakest link is the last—that in fact is the key leadership option. Although trying to make sense of why and how things went wrong is no easy or quick task—it will be studied for months or even years—it is essential for recovery. It is a natural follow-up to confession and precedes setting up paths to or plans for the future.

Minimally, CEOs have to acknowledge the profound difference of these tough times—that they are not the same old, same old. They depart from the business and economics as usual. The frameworks, scale, and players are new and intimidating. Finally, not only has the game changed but for many it also threatens to be an endgame. In short, deciding to try to make sense of the why and the wherewithal of hard times creates the necessary design threshold for reinvention.

Revisioning

Hard times also tap the birth pangs of the future. More than any other factor, they compel visioning or rather re-visioning. But not old platitudes. They require, at minimum, the following:

- The forces of discontinuity and globality have to be permanently built in as driving factors.
- Contingency has to structure strategic planning.
- Wild cards have to be considered norms.
- Hard times usher in a brave new world the likes of which we have never seen before.
- The call for creative leaders has never been clearer and more needed than ever before.

- A new vision and combination of savvy and smarts has to leverage a brave new world of innovation.
- And if all or enough of that happens, then tough times may be the best investment for the future we ever made.

Exposing Excess—Pinpointing Failure

As a number of commentators have noted, transformational leaders following past great types have gone overboard and are guilty of the excess of hubris. For monsters like Stalin and Hitler, who built up a cult of hero worship so that they could do no wrong, whatever they said was the gospel and whatever they ordered done, no matter how hideous, was carried out. In fact, the transformational leader is the only one portrayed as a pseudo-leader who has misapplied his charisma for personal or outrageous gain. Often intelligence is corrupted first and becomes the evil genius capable of developing equally diabolical plans of destruction or embezzlement.

When the above converge, the failure is deep and almost genetic, and it is accompanied by exposure of excessive pay and bonuses essentially for incompetence, then the call goes out for change—total, top to bottom, but always starting with the top as the supreme example. The mandate for change thus is so absolute that it refuses the compromise of the tried and experienced hand, lest that carry with it the old ways that have brought about the demise in the first place.

Crisis thus becomes the supreme opportunity for the emergence of the leader of change. Embracing the perception of being a deliverer or savior, this new advocate of change often applies such salvationist leverage to clear the way or silence all opposition or time-servers. Then we wait—during the proverbial one hundred days or less if we are desperate—to see what change hath wrought, whether the deliverer hath delivered, and whether we are being brought to the new promised land.

Cheered on to failure, the changer is always going up a down escalator, facing odds never in his favor, encountering excessive expectations of being a miracle worker. And suddenly he stops and grins and swells because he has been waiting his entire life to be this kind of heady leader and to be remembered for taking on the whole nine yards when no one else was chosen to be the leader of the pack. And he loves every minute of it.

Looking a Gift Horse in the Mouth

But perhaps the most sensational example of the difference of the transformational leader is his rejection of conventional solutions of success. Such is the case with the current explanations of superior workforce performance.

Stretch goals have become such a basic and permanent part of the work environment that job descriptions not only are regularly exceeded, but also often outdated. The objection "That is not in my job description!" is met with the ultimate catch-22 last line: "And all other duties as may be required or assigned." As a result, doing whatever it takes has become the new work mantra. But it is often punitive—"And if you can't do it, I will find someone who can!"—or abandoning—"I can't tell you what to do. You have to figure it out yourself."

But given the steady gains in productivity, employees and managers evidently are figuring it out and doing whatever it takes to keep their jobs as well as getting the job done. After awhile, we even tend to take that for granted, accept it as the new work ethic norm, and routinely are manipulative to achieve or surpass such stretch results.

Theoretically there seems to be no limit to upping the ante. In fact, frequently, middle-level managers are charged with finding new ways to squeeze even more productivity out of the same number of people and operations. And then all can sit back and enjoy the windfall of accomplishing more or the same amount with less and taking credit for the law of supply and demand going our way.

And yet, to some, the situation requires more analysis, especially by transformational HR directors and CEOs. They have paused to examine the dynamics of the process because transformation is their mission. Above all, what seems most puzzling is that the gains have come about on their own, automatically and without any executive or HR intervention. Since clearly the impacts are profound, there is a strong interest in what is driving the process, whether it will continue, and, if not, what can be salvaged or what can be substituted to continue meeting stretch goals.

Five questions quickly surface:

1. Is this display of worker talent and potential a basic HR factor?
2. If not, what is?
3. Is fear the basic motivational driver of productivity?
4. Why are job descriptions so prescriptively limiting?
5. Can they be revised to accommodate different levels of achievement and expectation?

In the process, internal and external possibilities begin to appear. Can something more supportive, interventionist, and even empowering be internally added if such gains and morale are to be maintained? And can it also carry over and be applied externally to the challenge of new hires?

Job descriptions are basic to such a change process. They establish job essentials, serve as benchmarks for evaluation, and are needed for legal and posting purposes. To be sure, given current work environments, they require updating, although each adjustment might be negated or supplanted by the need for constantly new adjustments.

But still there is value to the basic uniformity of work descriptions across an industry. If change then is to occur, the baby cannot be thrown out with the bath water. It should supplement and not replace job descriptions, but it needs to be as generic as the current last line. That way all contingences and applications would be covered. It also has to apply to all holders of that position and to all the challenges that may confront them now, next week, and forever. Above all, it must be worker-activated and empowered.

Increasingly, there is a need to build into job descriptions precisely the challenge not only of job flexibility, but also of job transformation. To get the job done needs the supplement of changing the job if that is what it takes. But such an initiative should be both explicitly identified and invited from the outset as a form of self-directed job development. Every job description thus would come with the expectation to change the job in order to get it done. That would mean that every job description is intentionally unfinished; it is a work in progress. Its up-to-date status and versions are in the hands and heads of job holders.

What are the advantages and benefits of supplementing description with expectation?

- It is neither punitive nor abandoning.
- It becomes an up-front, no-surprises job requirement.
- It puts the employee in the driver's seat.
- Job definition is made an opportunity not just a responsibility.
- It offers the ownership of empowerment.
- It is routinely proactive.
- Documenting job change supports performance.

Such a supplement can thus function as a built-in, self-generated, and self-fulfilling prophecy. But it also can be tapped for further gains. To optimize, extend, and reinforce its reverberating potential, two additional avenues might be considered.

The first is that job expectation provides the key access to the intervention of managerial mentoring. The focus on job change and transformation is ready-made for the supportive process of coaching such change. In addition, the documentation required now brings new rigor and precision to the job evaluation process itself.

Now performance is perceived not solely as a series of past and present stills but as an ongoing unfinished process inviting later development. The future becomes the job's new partner, linking continuous growth with job projection. And with the priority of employee-driven documentation, performance evaluation now becomes a shared, and not a unilateral, exchange. Wired in place and made a prominent part of the hiring challenge and orientation, such a job supplement has the potential to support and acculturate new hires to the company culture of ad infinitum change.

Another intervention focuses on building a culture of shared work expectations. It should celebrate change as a company-wide goal and mission. Such performance redefinition might benefit from dissemination by being ritualized as a public event. Every three months or so company-wide sharing of job change should take place. Otherwise, both its commonality and variety might be lost and its collective impacts unacknowledged, untapped, and uninspiring. Minimally, it should occur on a department and divisional basis. The presentations would be based on the documentation already in hand suitably stripped of names and titles. No matter how small or merely incremental, the emphasis would be not only on how each initiative contributes to the overall impact but also on how the knowledge of individual job change can set up a chain reaction for other work revisions. Special attention would be paid to divisional overlap. Profiles of such job and role changes also would be collected and aggregated upward, especially those of divisional cross-overs. Overall, company-wide patterns would appear. The net result hopefully would be the recognition of an emerging work culture focused on the future of job enhancement.

The value of supplementing description with expectation is that it is both reassuring and empowering. It normalizes doing whatever it takes with the new option of changing the job—perhaps everyday, ever so slightly, but collectively and constantly. Companies can thus change, not only from within but also from without. Attracting new talent can be both facilitated and customized when HR can offer the challenge of work leadership as a shared job expectation turned over to those who have to do it. Finally, wiring in place job expectation also provides the rare opportunity to fuse and align mission and vision on both an individual and company-wide basis and to do so by impacting the bottom line.

How often does change of such scope and depth come our way? The answer is that it does not. It is created by transformational leaders who in the process of questioning a gift horse in the mouth discover a mother lode of change. And when and while its potential and applications for workforce improvement take place, the transformational leader feeling his oats asks, "Okay, what is next?"

The overall context for all leadership types appears in the five categories summarized in table 15.1.

Table 15.1. Leadership Types Summary

Role	Focus	Outcomes	Direction
1. The Changer	Transformation	New Vision	Vertical
2. The Rearranger	Transactional	New Structures	Horizontal
3. The Integrator	Holistic	New Composites	Lateral/Zig-Zag
4. The Anticipator	Leapfrogging	New Cyborgs	Out Front/Ahead
5. The Innovator	Inventive	New Culture	Circular

Zeroing in on the transformational leader, what follows is an elaborated version of the roles he plays.

Profile of the Changer

Roles
The Climber
The Driver
The Lone Ranger
Type-A Personality
Action-Oriented
Gut Instinct
Workaholic
One-Man Show
Takes Over Everything
All Is Grist for the Mill of Change
Genius Leadership
Great Man Leadership
Big Idea
Indispensable
The Savior

The transformational leader looms large. He is bigger than life, one of a kind, and a miracle worker. He appears tireless and everywhere. A one-man show, his intelligence turns everything upside down and inside out as his mercurial analysis and evaluation determines whether it is grist for the mill of change. He proceeds through a company like Sherman marching through Georgia, department by department, level by level, until nothing remains unexamined, intact, or unaltered. After a while, no one even remembers what was initially there. Old published manuals of operations and procedures are discarded and now can be found in documents on the web, which are endlessly edited and revised.

Focus
Review and Eliminate
Alter to Align

Shape Up or Resign
Our Way or the Highway
Get with the Program
Energy and Enthusiasm
Leave Nothing Intact
Driven toward Excellence

The transformational leader has zero tolerance for the old ways of doing things and is determined to drag this relic (kicking and screaming
if necessary) into the twenty-first century. No respecter of tradition or
the nostalgia of past success or the ways it was delivered before, all he
relentlessly asks is whether it meets current metrics. And if it does, woe
to any unit or professional that gets in the way of salvation and does
not get with the program. They appropriately are named "History!"

Modes
Rallying
Cheerleading
Inspirational Retreats
Bonuses for Winners
A Star System
Loyalty
CEO Knows Best
Endless Improvement
Balanced Score Card

The transformational leader loves to keep score, maintain constantly
and update his brag book and pause regularly to cheerlead and celebrate and single out those who are winners like him, send them to
Hawaii, and hail them: "If I had fifty like these, I could transform not
just this company but also the entire industry overnight!"

Direction
Upward
No End in Sight
Sky Is the Limit
Highest ROI

Industry Leader
Hierarchical
Pyramidal
Chain of Command

Basically a vertical leader, he supports the chain of command and the eternal hierarchy of the pyramid. He knows no other way of achieving unity of purpose and clarity of command. Professionals get their marching orders. Marketing is a campaign with attack segments. Strategic planning anticipates and counters the efforts of the enemy. He is the general as CEO. He takes no prisoners.

Outcomes
New Stirring Vision of Company
Branded Excellence
Measuring Transformation
Before and After
Celebration of Growth/Change
Next Ten-Year Plan
"Ain't Seen Nothing Yet!"

The transformer is a producer, a maker, a creator across the board. The bottom line shows a surplus each year; ROI is favorable and stockholders are happy; and sales and productivity have been posted every year. To be sure, we now have an employee union brought about by failures of due process in firing or reassigning workers. But that has been dealt with. Every three years a new contract has to be negotiated, but that too is manageable and has not stopped the momentum. Above all, we have a new company with a new vision. Its future mandate for excellence is accompanied by the CEO proclaiming, "You ain't seen nothing yet!"

Although the strokes above may be a bit broad and the rendition at times one dimensional, the portrait of the transformer generally rings true and is reminiscent not only of the giants of both the nineteenth and twentieth centuries but also of the twenty-first and the legacy of icons like Lee Iacocca, Fred Smith, and Jack Welch. Hero and leadership worship are finally alike.

But what is missing is a separate and detailed examination of how the transformer makes such accomplishments happen—so much so that what can be posited is the existence of transformational intelligence, as distinct and identifiable as the leadership type it supports and helps to flourish. To be sure that also means that each leadership type possesses its own brand of intelligence that is distinctive and learnable. Indeed, one of the key ways of becoming such a leader is to acquire that intelligence and allow it gradually to take the lead of your command and vision center.

Here then is a profile of some of the key dimensions of transformational intelligence.

Student of History

No other leadership type is as absorbed or obsessed about history and even ancient sacred texts. The transactional leader has only passing interest; the innovative leader almost none; the anticipatory leader uses it as a benchmark; the integrative leader identifies rare instances of a da Vinci. Not surprisingly, then, this supreme changer of change puts his intelligence to the historical task.

What does he hope to find? Enviable examples of great empires and great heroes. Even Jesus and God are retrofitted to emerge as ancient-modern CEOs. In other words, there is much to choose from because history and scripture essentially was written about and from the point of view of great men.

But what was the key lesson? Transformation—all the great leaders struggled to bring about change and deal with stiff-necked, obstinate people always looking backward and preferring the comfort of slavery to the headiness of freedom. It all reads like a modern text and case study. No wonder modern leaders behave like Moses or Caesar—why they turn to history and find it so reassuring and affirming of their role; why adapting the role of a prophet gives new urgency to their vision; and how it is possible to convert the notion of the promised land into a deliverable.

To be sure, history also generates a lesson many transformational leaders seek to ignore, namely, that of demise. Great empires rise but they also fall, and it happens so regularly and across nations, cultures, and time that endgames seem to be inevitably the common fate of even spectacular start-ups.

But such unwillingness to accept termination is characteristic of the willfulness of transformational leaders and their faith that intelligence will find a way out and around such a common fate. In short, the ultimate role of transformational intelligence is to exempt this worshipper of history from laws of history.

Structures—Pyramids

If ever history could claim one direction over all the others, it would be that of the vertical. Pyramidal and ascending, it embodies hierarchy and order. It enshrines empires, religions, and organizational charts. It is the epitome of bureaucracy, always busy putting one layer above another, one ruler or supervisor over rank and file, and in the process justifying itself by establishing orderly succession up the ladder. An entrepreneur would be a misfit in this vertical world, and if he survived he would be forced to fit in. But the chain of command is absolute and unforgiving.

Indeed, vertical leaders believe professionals and companies need such challenges to stir and get the juices flowing and to realize their performance potential—of what they can be and do. They also believe they uniquely have the capacity to develop a vision to achieve such distinction and the inspiration to motivate what it takes to get there. The vertical is thus inevitably the favored choice of the transformational leader, who in fact needs size and reluctance to demonstrate his transformation power and whose charisma has to be sufficient and stirring enough to win and carry the day.

Such leaders are compulsive changers. Everything and everyone is grist for the mill of total transformation. The given, the inherited, the status quo all invite the wrecking ball of cleaning house. If the eighteenth-century watchword was "Whatever Is, Is Right," the twenty-first claimed "Whatever Is, Is to Be Changed"—irrevocably, forever. The plan is clear: rebuild the world in the image of change (and the changer) until piece by piece it becomes a totally new creation. What then? Move on to the next calling—to the next dinosaur structure that requires a complete new sweep and breath of fresh air.

But lest one conclude that the vertical is solely the monopoly of transformational leaders and inevitably accompanied by bravado and rallying slogans, there are some quieter and more analytical signs that, as a leadership pathway, it is being chosen for reasons that are somewhat at variance with its more rigid and hierarchical history. The overall direction remains vertical but now moves not only up but also down, courts not only the heights but also the depths. There the transactional supplements the transformational, the situational supplements the visionary, as transformation and vision become not the sole objects of leadership but are replaced or forced to share the stage with the less glamorous but persuasive nature of process.

Charisma is now tamed and paired with analysis. In other words, the image of the commanding leader does not disappear as he becomes less official and more dispensable—not so much a star on the stage but a guide on the side. But the telltale sign that the vertical leader is not changing his spots appears in the characteristic problem-solving methodology he chooses. In fact, one of the recurrent leadership patterns is the strong preference not only for how he solves problems but also for how he communicates.

Communications

We still tend to pay attention to changer-leaders who are different—who set themselves apart by what they do, what they say, and often by how they act and think. We particularly value those who are not bland or inhabit the shadows. We prefer the visible, assertive, and vigorous who are knowledgeable about their business and industry, speak their minds, explain their decisions, and do not play it safe or indulge in predictable platitudes but openly are champions.

At their best they combine savvy and smarts, but they do not claim to be geniuses or parade their high IQ. Besides, as Fred Smith, CEO of FedEx, has wisely reminded us, the outstanding violinist or top hitter probably would not make the best conductor or coach. In other words, the determiner is not performance but leading performance. And again and again that is their distinction. They love to be out front and in charge, they cherish the affirmation of followers, and they work hard and long. When asked for advice, they typically claim that leading is learnable; it is a craft, a skill, and a style and it is also addictive. But preeminently it is always actionable. It is in the doing, especially in the doing of things differently and creatively. That trait, when added to two others, forms the leadership trinity: the ability to read the times, to remain unfinished, and to do things differently.

We are accustomed to regard the forces around us as not of our own making—as a given of history. Our task is somehow to make sense of what we have inherited and play the hand dealt to us. But that is not what vertical leaders do. They do not accept the given. Instead, they read the times. They do not regard anything as immutable or fixed in stone. They test, they probe, and they turn things on their head. And they do so by being doers. They don't understand any other way. To them reality is a contest to see who comes out on top, which vision prevails, and which company survives, grows, and outlasts the others.

The ultimate way they view their role as a leader is neither as a time server nor a passive observer of the passing scene. Instead, the leader is a constant combatant who never ignores challenges, leaves anything intact or unmet, and who aggressively, confidently, and quietly goes about the business of being smarter and more imaginative than the competition. If in the process the leader is able to persuade others not only to follow his lead but also to add their unique gifts to the repertoire of doing things differently, then he is justified being in charge and earning the big bucks: "How far and fast do we have to go just to catch up, let alone get ahead?"

And can we form helpful alliances along the way, as suggested in the next chapter?

Transformational and Servant Leadership: An Odd Couple?

S ENIOR MANAGERS WHO HAVE SERVED under powerful leaders maintain that the company is not the same. But how can that be? Are CEOs still that dominating? How can their leadership style become company culture? And have we generally overlooked the telltale signs that warn us in advance of a legacy of substantial, incremental, and even discontinuous organizational change the CEO leaves behind? What should we be looking for in the proverbial first one hundred days after a leader assumes command that is predictive of what is to come? There are at least five subtle signs to note.

Thinking

How does the CEO think? Is he slow, deliberate or fast; big picture or snapshot; present or future oriented? Does he get impatient with those who think differently? How does he show his pleasure or displeasure? Does the selection of his senior team serve to mirror or contrast his thinking style?

We are often so preoccupied with external results that we have little interest in the thought processes that were involved in making the original decision. As a result, we pay a great deal of attention to implementation rather than conceptualization. A company should not hire a CEO that is an intellectual lightweight. The capacity for powerful conceptualization is only a step away from powerful leadership.

Starting Points

How and where does he typically start things off? What are his recurrent first questions? Does he characteristically offer or ask for background or history? How important is the past to him? Or does he prefer to plunge right into the middle of things—*in media res*—and then move ahead quickly? Does he ever accept interruptions when he is holding forth or pause and seek reflective feedback at critical points?

Many leaders lead by the example of illustrative stories or life-changing experiences. Everything is suspended while a dramatic tale is told that clinches and sums up the argument and pulls together all the pieces and ties up loose ends. The process also may be surprising when other matters or areas are suddenly brought into play as the CEO expands the parameters of the discussion. Finally, he may frequently reframe so that, as the return to the original track takes place, it may be both more inclusive and consensual. In other words, is how and where he starts with certain subjects expansive or restricted, inviting or excluding?

Ending Points

Are his conclusions arrived at cumulatively or sequentially? Does he incorporate opposing positions or are they deleted in his summation? Is he always hot to trot and poised for action? Is he always calling for what's next? Do his conclusions tick off a detailed checklist or are they a rapid and sweeping flourish? Does he take the time to relate all the parts and preserve all? Does he value the whole as a spawning context? And then does he concern himself with follow-up—how are we going to make this happen?—or parcel out and delegate the final communication and implementation of a decision to others?

Priorities and Preferences

What does he like and dislike doing? What gets his juices flowing and his heart pumping? What does he seem to just endure? Does he like to fight? Will he sit for hours going over and over the details and be totally absorbed to the oblivion of everything and everyone else? Is he happy, moody, or angry most of the time? What makes his energy level rise or fall? Is he steady or mercurial? Does he like crossword puzzles?

Ego

How important is it for him to be *numero uno* and be acknowledged as such by all? How does he react to praise? Does he swell or appear uncomfortable? Is he easily bruised or hurt? Is it more important for him to succeed or for the company to succeed? What is his driving mission in life? What legacy if any does he seek to leave? Does he consider himself so indispensable that he thinks without him the company will fall apart? Does he thank others?

One could go on, but I think the point has been made. We need to recognize the power of leadership style to influence the imitative behaviors of senior staff and to shape company culture. Therefore, we need to choose wisely. We need to supplement the interview process for CEOs by raising more internal and indirect questions of leadership dynamics and style once we have determined what we want and what will make the organization flourish. We also have to factor in what kind of CEO style may be needed at a particular point in the evolution of the organization.

The key then is hiring or working with a CEO who has considerable conceptual power (grasp of the situation); values background (knows the score and the competition, starts and ends in a unified way, and dots the i's and crosses the t's); loves to solve problems, especially in a creative way (models innovation and out-of-the-box thinking); and blends his identity with that of the company (vision and mission are one and the same).

The last point is a major commitment of servant leadership and raises the interesting prospect of an alliance or even a fusion of transformation and Robert Greenleaf's leadership advocacy. Leaders are defined and measured in various ways: results, leadership qualities, decisiveness, innovation, and so forth. In *The Power of Servant Leadership*, Greenleaf put service at the top of the list because he claims that is the way to achieve all of the above and more: "One test of any kind of leadership is: Do leaders enjoy a mutual relationship with followers?" (119). He goes on to argue that the critical task of effective leaders is managing serving relationships. Servant-leaders are charged with finding commonality, coherence, and consensuality as the means of holding relationships between leaders and followers together. The common ground between leaders and followers consists of power, focus, initiatives, and decisiveness. The dynamic is how the four are sorted out between the two.

Greenleaf claims that there are basically three models of relationships between leaders and followers. The first is the unidirectional or unilateral model; the second the negotiated or shared model; and the third the mutual model. A visual version and discussion of each appears below.

Unidirectional or Unilateral Model

This model flows in only one direction, from leader to follower as it passes through the four areas:

Leader—Power—Focus—Initiatives—Decisiveness—*Followers*

Here the chain of command and implementation goes only one way. Nothing is shared. Power derives from the leader. It is a singular and not a multiple line passing through and connecting all four areas. Followers learn of what is expected of them by announcements and pronouncements, not through discussion. Advice or concurrence is not sought or given.

This is a perfect model for a results-driven organization, although to achieve those gains working environments may be punitive. If the CEO is an outstanding Attila the Hun and if the market for the products or services is favorable, the organization will post significant gains and pay a handsome return on investment.

Negotiated or Shared Model

The accommodation between leaders and followers is brought about by cooperative and adversarial negotiation. In the first instance, leaders and followers develop more cooperative relationships because of the common need to achieve certain gains and because the special style and vision of the leader eliminates the mentality of them and

Table 16.1. Cooperative Power Structure between Leaders and Followers

LEADERS	Power Focus Initiative Decisiveness	FOLLOWERS

us. On the outside, business may be at war, but inside the organization business is peace. If unions are involved, hard negotiations may have produced this shared model. But it tends to be precarious, contested, and regularly open to sudden interventions by shop stewards.

Unlike the first singular model, which enforces uniformity in all four areas, the shared model may be uneven. The extent or degree of the sharing varies with each of the four areas and the degree of leadership commitment to partnership. Although the leadership may be directed more toward liberalizing rather than controlling relationships, how much also depends on where the company is at in its history and evolution. If the goal is innovation, a top-down approach is usually ineffective. Creativity cannot be coerced. The shared model might be more successful in encouraging all employees to be essentially the company's R&D.

The Mutual Model
Leaders/Followers
Followers/Leaders
Power—Focus—Initiatives—Decisiveness

The mutual model is totally collaborative. Leaders and followers develop a reciprocal relationship; they may even exchange roles. This goes beyond cooperation to their becoming co-creative in all four areas. Greenleaf claims that such an organization can produce results, motivate innovation, and embody a vision of service. Indeed, the relationship between leaders and followers is essentially one of mutual service to each other, with the net result being the creation of Greenleaf's supreme organizational vision, the servant institution.

But such an institution and such a model of mutuality cannot be assumed or merely proclaimed. It has to be built. Above all, the model has to be learned and communicated. In other words, the servant-leader has two tasks: building and learning the craft of commonality and developing the communication of consensuality.

Building and Learning Mutuality

Greenleaf employs four building blocks to establish a relationship of mutuality between leader and followers: develop people, sustain equal exchange between them, seek and create consensus, and reduce uncertainty.

"Develop Everyone You Touch"

The servant-leader serves learning. But the learning is not just quantitative or incremental but qualitative and holistic. Greenleaf asks of a goal, "Does it have a healing or civilizing influence? Does it nurture the servant motive in people, favor their growth as persons, and help them distinguish those who serve from those who destroy?" (114–15). Thus, the learning must face both inward and outward. It has to have as one of its outcomes building a service culture within the organization. That is the only way to develop a customer service company.

Greenleaf pauses to comment on employees who do not always fit in and are outspoken. He calls them "seekers." Frequently critical, sometimes even off-the-wall types, they routinely question the status quo and the orthodoxy of the organization's way of doing things. They need to be protected and even cherished. An institution that is not big and flexible enough to accept mavericks is a fragile or rigid institution and not a learning organization. Then too often the special value of the seekers is embryonic. They may be emerging leaders in their own right. They also may embody a different future direction for the company. In any case, they dramatize the second building block: the interchangeability of leaders and followers.

Sustain Equality of Exchange

Greenleaf never supported pyramidal hierarchies. They were edifice complexes supporting excessive ego and separatism, the one being a version of the other. Today we might call them Towers of Enron. Such structures create too much distance between leaders and followers, especially for Greenleaf who seeks greater equality and commonality between them.

Greenleaf's argument starts from an assumption that the limits of executive power stem from the limits of executive knowledge. Leaders at the top do not know everything, about everything, all the time. They thus have to recognize that whatever edge they enjoy is temporary: "Even the ablest leaders will do well to be aware that there are times and places in which they should follow. And one who seems deficient in one or more of these qualities may . . . rise to save the day" (114).

Thus, the relationship of mutuality extends to the exchange of roles. Leaders will become followers and followers will become leaders when the combination of the need and the expertise are joined to require them to be equals. In fact, it might even be claimed that the assumption of that role by followers is the ultimate form of their professional and learning development. But such elevation to leadership by followers often needs the sanction of the CEO: "The titular leader gives continuity and coherence to an endeavor in which many may lead" (120).

The reciprocity of leaders and followers is not conditional on who has more and who has less. In other words, there is no giver and no taker. Both are both—"the more able and the less able serving each other." It cannot be otherwise because each needs what the other has for completion. The more able have to offer the perspective and knowledge that their moreness has to give, just as the less able have to define the need and contribution of having less. To do otherwise is to pass off a half as a whole. Genuine wholeness is born of reciprocal partnership and its ultimate achievement is always shared. One cannot grant wholeness to oneself. It comes out of a process of plus and minus, the more able and the less able, the mutuality of leaders and followers. They are co-creators, and rightly so, for as Greenleaf puts it, "There is something subtle communicated to one who is being served and led if, implicit in the compact between servant-leader and led, is the understanding that the search for wholeness is something they share" (8).

Create Consensus

The search for commonality is one that leaders and followers undertake together. The leader is a "consensus finder," a consensus creator, and a consensus articulator (138). "One leads by the concepts that will enlarge the number who find common ground. The leader thus strives to bring the people together, and hold them together, as an effective force" (138–39).

Effectiveness is an affirmation of commonality; it is the hoops that hold the barrel together. There is no need to lecture any group about the value of consensuality when it experiences directly its collective power. As Greenleaf notes, "There is nothing that builds organizational strength quite like a high order of consensus regarding goals and strategies" (105). But it is not that easy or automatic. There are obstacles to consensuality just as there are to mutuality.

Reduce Uncertainty

The biggest obstacle is the desire for certainty in excess of what the world can legitimately provide. The world is stingy as far as assurances are concerned. Similarly, problems exist for which there do not appear to be any solutions, creating the impression that collectively our problems are in excess of our capacity to solve them. Greenleaf recommends that we stop calling them problems and instead call them challenges, for they may be with us a long time and we may never be able to solve them. As challenges, we can continue to work together to manage, if not to solve, them (105). This is not mere semantics because as a consensus seeker Greenleaf is aware of what can prevent or compromise mutuality. In fact, "defusing the anxiety of people who want more certainty than exists in the situation" (125) is precisely the sign of a consensual leader.

The servant-leader has to reduce uncertainty because, until anxiety is calmed, common ground will not emerge. When the numbers sharing that common ground increase to a critical mass, a consensual culture in which the servant motive can thrive has been formed, and co-creation between leaders and followers can take place. But Greenleaf believes that uncertainty can be reduced and consensual cultures can thrive only when the right kind of communication is sustained between leaders and followers. And so his final admonition is to value the communication of commonality.

According to Greenleaf, the three communication modes, which are not unlike the three organizational structures noted above, are the coercive, manipulative, and persuasive. Each has its own base of power and its own way of modeling relationships.

Coercive

Greenleaf's analysis of coercive power obviously follows the highly directive structure of the first model of unilateral relationships, but, at the same time, it deals with subtler forms of coercion, masking itself under noble ideals. For example, Greenleaf cites the credentialing power of universities, which in the name of high standards force students into being certified in only certain ways. Few regard universities or similar bodies that prescribe or dictate credentials as coercive, as they appear noble in their regard for safeguarding social institutions. However, the only reason that they can play that self-appointed protective role is because they have the power to do so.

Manipulative

Manipulative power and communication, in contrast, do not use sanctions or threats or pressures but rather plausible explanations that in fact do not really explain anything. Greenleaf claims that many leaders come to decisions and then seek to find plausible explanations for what was basically intuitive. But when the decision is in excess of the rational explanations, followers may feel manipulated, even duped. However, because of the availability of superior informational sources at the top, employees are cowed into concluding that they do not know enough to judge and therefore have to go along with the executive decision. But those who are savvier, or have watched this manipulative game being played many times, begin to be suspicious and ask, "Okay, what is the hidden agenda this time?"

A leader pays a high price for his shortcuts by damaging long-term relationships. Or, in Greenleaf's words, "manipulation hangs as a cloud over the relationship between leader and led almost everywhere, and is the subject of much pejorative comment" (85). In short, manipulation involves passing off a half as a whole, not telling the truth, the whole truth, and nothing but the truth. When that occurs, as it does regularly in the world of the second model of relationships, adversarial forces are activated and begin to press for a less manipulative, more direct communication and relationships.

Persuasive

Clearly, Greenleaf favors persuasion because it is based on and at the heart of mutuality. Greenleaf begins by claiming that persuasion is initially and finally an internal process. "One is persuaded, I believe, upon the arrival at a feeling of rightness about a belief or action through one's own intuitive sense" (85).

Leaders thus do not have a monopoly on intuition. Indeed, it is critical for them to recognize that all their followers are also intuitive because then both leader and follower can understand and even agree on what conscious logic can and cannot offer. When that logic falls short, intuition may have to be the deciding factor.

But in a consensual culture it does not end there. Further efforts must be made over time to fill in the gaps. The decision may have been made but the need to complete the partial rationale, in other words, is still ongoing. Only that way can the leader keep the faith and bring that communication home and full. Thus, "both leader and follower respect the autonomy and integrity of the other and each allows and encourages the other to find his or her intuitive confirmation of the rightness of the belief or action" (85). In addition to having an immediate confirmatory effect, it also stores up trust for the future: "If this relationship prevails . . . when a quick action is required, one supported by the skimpiest of rationalizations, it will be accepted with the assurance that at some future time there will be the opportunity for intuitive mutuality to be reestablished" (85–86).

Greenleaf describes how the mutuality of persuasion is employed finally by followers: "A leader who practices persuasion whenever possible sets a model that, in time, will encourage followers to deal with the leader by persuasion. Power is generated in this relationship because it admits of mutual criticism, spirited arguments can occur, and it does not depend on artful stratagems" (86).

In summary, then, a relationship of mutuality offers much. It structures relationships between leaders and followers along lines of equality and reciprocity. Leaders can lean on followers. They also know that their role is clear: to develop everyone they touch to the point where the relationship of mutuality becomes more intuitive, spirited, and collaborative. The reciprocal relationship is managed through the notion of first among equals, especially modeled at the top, so that all are convinced that, at any given time, the best people are at the helm for however long that works.

Once again leaders do not have to work so hard at being indispensable, on the one hand, or 360 degrees, on the other. But in three major respects leaders have to be assertive. First, they have to be tireless consensus finders and persuaders, each being a path to the other. The ultimate achievement of servant leadership is thus the creation and maintenance of a consensual and persuasive culture. Second, the vision of a company is entrusted to and kept alive by the reciprocity of leaders and followers. Or, to quote Greenleaf's favorite Tao proverb, "When the leaders lead well the people think they did it themselves." Three, they may even have to form alliances with troublemakers.

Taming/Training Troublemakers   **17**

RECENTLY, I WAS INVOLVED IN A fascinating consulting challenge. An organization sought my advice on how to deal with excessive creativity. That was a new one for me. Most companies complain of its lack. What was equally puzzling was the perception that this was a problem. To say the least, it was intriguing.

The company was a recent amalgam. It was three organizations put together by a venture capital group to fill both a traditional and e-business market niche. The business plan that I reviewed was solid, as was the market analysis. The CEO and senior staff were experienced and seemed equal to the task of integrating the three cultures. The employees, both carry-overs and new hires, seemed impressive. Most important, it was working. All operational goals were met in the first year. By the second, profitability was lower than expected because of some unexpected and substantial cost increases. Corrective action had to be taken to ensure cash flow. The more innovative projects scheduled to be implemented in the third and fourth year were put on hold.

The reaction by the professional staff was not just strong but almost mutinous. For the most part they were entrepreneurs and had functioned on and off as independent contractors. They were risk takers. They had been hired with the understanding of profit sharing. Each employee was vested upon being hired and assigned a designated percentage share of earnings over and above salary. Moreover, such bonuses were to be separately given by a nonprofit foundation and research institute for tax purposes. In short, they saw their get-rich prospects decline and in some cases disappear. And they were furious. Their solution? Infusion of more capital to absorb any losses and maintain solvency. But do not change the growth plan. Do not alter what brought them all here in the first place. Move aggressively forward. Fearful of wholesale departures, on the one hand, and extensive counter-productivity, on the other, a major consulting firm was brought in to address the problem and to ease the transitions deemed necessary. Their initial contract was for six months, but, by the end of the first month, they threw their hands up in despair.

The consultants found the employees brilliant but impossible to work with. They were all prima donnas. They were narcissistic and seemed incapable of working together. Each one had an exalted view of his own genius and indispensability. Above all, they were all disturbers of the peace. They did not even stay within their own divisions but roamed and poached and pouted. Nothing was getting done. They challenged and baited each other endlessly like spoiled children. They would "yes, but" you to exhaustion. Recommendation: fire the lot and replace them with more docile creative types.

When that recommendation leaked out, one mischievous group, who called themselves "The Troublemakers" and who were clearly able to work together (at least in protest), decided to put together a list of criteria HR should use for the new hires. Secretly circulated, it was put in the form of a Q&A quiz (shown in table 17.1).

The following postscript was added to this quiz: "None of the present members of the non-solving and non-understanding consul-

Table 17.1.   Hiring Quiz

Questions	Typical Docile Answers	Creative Responses
1. Things are right or wrong?	Yes	Yes, no, and maybe.
2. Technology is good or bad?	Yes	Both, but it is also never neutral.
3. Teams are always smarter?	Yes	But when they blunder . . . look out.
4. Info-sharing is good?	Of course	But who owns the data?
5. Customer is always right?	Absolutely	No, but that is the challenge.

tant team brought in here to 'solve' us would ever come up with these questions, let alone the right answers." When the consulting team learned about the quiz and the postscript, they renegotiated the last five months of their contract and left in a huff. Their parting comment was that they did not want to be associated with failure.

I was brought in because I am comfortable with failure. I am still an on-and-off academic, and failure often provides more powerful grist for the seminar mill than success. I had no special reputation for pulling rabbits out of the hat where others couldn't. But I always had a fascination with and even weakness for creative types and how they function or fail to in corporate environments. In any case, the company was desperate. The first document the vice president of HR reluctantly gave me was the quiz. I was enormously impressed and said so, which rapidly increased his exasperation and led him to worry whether I was going to be part of the problem or the solution. He concluded that I probably was just like them and would only inflame the situation. He was half right; I was like them, but I was also mindful of my billables. I quickly made a mental note to pocket that quiz and use it sometime in a workshop on creativity.

A whole avalanche of questions poured in. Were these problems hangovers of some of the original cultures that went unresolved in the new amalgam? To what extent did bad times serve as a catalyst for bringing to the surface behaviors that previously were not problematic? Why did they call themselves "troublemakers"? That is such a strong, almost self-indicting term. Is that the role they saw themselves playing in the present situation or were they always that way, but masked by good times and the promise of prosperity? I had never encountered the term before in anything but a pejorative sense.

In any case, I became convinced then that my first task was to assemble a profile of good and bad aspects of being a troublemaker. Armed with that focus, I went into the enemy camp and listened to what the troublemakers had to say. And here is what I found:

- Troublemakers have been that way all their lives.
- They are round pegs forced into square holes.
- They take a perverse pride in not fitting in.
- They confessed that they were pains in the neck.

- They conceded they were the original "yes, but" types raised to an excruciating level.
- They enjoy being gadflies.
- They admitted to being destructive, constantly stalling groups or divisions from moving forward and accomplishing their tasks.
- But they were ultimately lovable and valuable.

It was even worse than I thought. In addition to all the above, I found them to be monomaniacs harping on the same thing over and over again. Nothing is ever simple. They make mountains out of mole hills. They are perfectionists. Nothing ever satisfies them. They seek endless revisions, reviews, and reengineering. They are exhausting.

But do they have any value? Begrudgingly, I say yes. They often have saved companies a great deal of embarrassment by pointing out that the emperor has no clothes. They always question assumptions. Their favorite phrase is "Where is it written that we have to do it this way?" They routinely stall the start of any project by asking seemingly endless questions: What does the current research show? What do we really know? And how do we know that? They constantly challenge the problem-solving process because of its predictable search for a solution proximate to the problem, whereas it may be hiding far away from the source of the difficulty. They also are compulsively futuristic. They devour science fiction and often believe organizations would be better off run on principles of science fiction. Unheeded, they would easily become whistleblowers and cheer every recall. They are annoyingly creative.

But although one may concede their occasional value, most colleagues and companies would wish them gone. Where? To a university where they could rightly and appropriately plague students or to a think tank where they could drive other troublemakers crazy.

Nevertheless, here was a rare opportunity—not just a few but a whole host of troublesome but nevertheless creative types. The starting point was unique. Instead of beginning with managers who were not innovative and getting them to embrace deviant thinking and creative dislocation, these people were already there. In other words, the task was to work backward. Instead of trying to make them creative, the aim was to civilize them without extinguishing the creative spark. Would it be possible to preserve the best but restrain the rest? Imagine being able to extract from the solitary troublemaker his or her positive essentials and adjust them for teamwork. Could that salvaged result in turn be turned around and used as a training model? Could those who are not troublemakers be trained to bring special value to organizations badly in need of assumptions analysis, restructuring, and innovation? The gains in thinking outside of the box could be considerable, especially if the exasperating downsides could be eliminated or reduced.

But I was getting ahead of myself; I needed to stay focused on the issue of striking a balance between contrariness and cooperation. Many were skeptical; some were convinced it could not be done or not without trade-offs at both ends that would jeopardize the worth of the outcome. Certainly, the task was formidable and the odds daunting. I searched for already existing models or, more properly, a combination of those models that had been successful in their own right but not been converged and integrated to focus on the task of building a collaborative troublemaker. I was convinced that I had to limit my focus. I did not wish to take on the problems of structures or cultures. And I certainly did not wish to address financial issues. My instinct told me that whatever peace and turn-around could be brought to this situation required taking head-on the challenge of creating collaborative troublemakers rather than trying to get rid of them. Toward that end, there were three role models I thought might be pressed into service: the researcher, the consultant, and the trusted advisor.

Each model brings something special and even urgent to the creation of a professional. The researcher is preeminently a problem poser and definer. The consultant is preeminently a problem solver, a challenger of basic assumptions, and an uncompromising advocate. The trusted advisor articulates the conscience of a corporation, its integrity, and its humanity.

But here everything had to start from a different starting point. Typically, employees involved in creativity training and learning are not malcontents. They are reasonably bright, open, and balanced. To be sure, they also are at a point where they may unknowingly be complacent or stuck. They may have stopped short of getting to the next plateau. Such states of inertia typically will not respond to the standard training incremental fare. Instead, what they may need is a jump-start—something discontinuous, a leap forward, a break in the predictable pattern—to get their attention.

Indeed, the outcomes being sought required changing the way we perceive, examine, and relate to things, people, and situations. To possess pivotal value, the reformed troublemaker's output had to be corrective on the one hand and liberating on the other. The goal was to produce a totally different working arrangement and community. That involved creating their own working environment, which was to be self-designed, self-maintained, and self-governing, with no one in charge. Their basic obligations were to each other and to the project. They were totally inward facing. They wanted to ignore the rest of the company and its rules of behavior and dress, especially of working hours and days and access to labs, offices, or studios. They wanted 24/7 access. They were completely in charge; a huge program board that monitored project progress was mounted on the east wall. Prayers and meditation sessions could be scheduled any time or day of the week and would never be regarded as an interruption. A padded tantrum room was reserved outside the work area. But increasingly it was used as a retreat and meditative space. It was named the Buddha room.

Although the expectations of change were substantial, they were not unreachable. If the training was to take hold, those involved would not emerge as new or unrecognizable but rather recast. Above all, the exposure to the roles of researcher, consultant, and trusted advisor were not abstract but company and project specific. Each employee in other words was asked to apply the principles of each model to his own style and to real in-house problems.

Did the training work? Yes. And did it take and last? Yes. Did it in fact civilize the troublemakers? Beyond our wildest expectations. Why was it successful? I had my own explanations, but, at the last workshop meeting, which unsurprisingly they took over, the now collaborative mavericks described what to each of them moved their transformations. Here is a sample:

- "We were not told what to do or become. A finished product was not held up as a template. It was all in our hands. Good thing too. What we produced was brilliant."

- "They were great models to contemplate. I never thought of myself as being a consultant and therefore an advocate. The trusted advisor role blew my mind. I imagined myself working with our CEO. Except now I would not so much be telling him what to do but drawing him out; hopefully leading him down a more humane path. But to do that I really had to practice self-restraint because I already had all the right answers."
- "I loved the prospect of being a consultant. I am a permanent student. I pride myself on being unfinished. I have the feeling I could give myself a PhD. But what stopped me in my tracks was methodology. I recognized that I would have to design my own way through to an answer. I had always left that to institutions, which is so totally unlike me."
- "I was amazed by the variety and diversity. We all thought we were all unique. And happily that did not change. But we were sealed within ourselves. We never understood or appreciated the hot stuff of others. And in a couple of exercises in which we had to work together, wow, five of us left the earth."
- "I was worried all the time that we would be tamed and come out dull. But we had a great lion tamer who let us roar and jump when we wanted to. After a while we even forgot we were in a cage."
- "I have always been a pain in the neck, too smart and big for my britches. I found out I don't have to be a pain to be smart. All I have to be is a cooperative troublemaker. It hurt!"

All believed that they had created a new culture of collaborative disagreement for the company. They embraced the tough discipline of each role in a unique way, harmonized it with their difference, and internalized a new whole. The problem-solving formats and confidential dialogue protocols they produced were all masterful, intriguing, and often uniquely usable. Above all, it was wonderful to observe them now as part of a questioning culture that is principled, purposeful, productive, and innovative. And also happily, routinely civil—occasionally. But they would never make peace with the everyday demands of transactional types.

18

THE REARRANGER

OVERCOMING LIMITS IS A recurrent obsession, especially of managerial leadership. "Limits" does not mean what leaders are unable or fail to do because of ineptitude, indecisiveness, or miscalculation. Rather, it is what they should not be doing, even though they have the capacity to do it.

Such inhibitions may appear to be a strange course of action to recommend. After all, managers are hired precisely because of what they can do and what needs to be done, hopefully a marriage and fit made in heaven. And historically that is the way it has been. But there is too much at stake now and in the future for that course of action to tap the increasing independence and interdependence of the workforce.

The psychologists tell us that, if you don't allow and encourage children to do things on their own, especially if it seems to take them excruciatingly long, and parents interfere to hasten completion, they may grow up to be managers in organizations who routinely do not complete their tasks, fail to dot the i's and cross the t's, miss deadlines, and can't delegate. In fact, our experts of course have a name for it: completion deficiency.

Organizations need to create room not at the top but at the middle and at the bottom. But that can't happen with a management that is too invasive, too intrusive, too relentlessly needed. If the increasing independence of the workforce is to be affirmed and advanced, then increased space and place for employees to be decision-makers, innovative thinkers, and future-driven actors needs to be provided. To accomplish this, the following non-steps should be taken by managers.

Step Back

Don't always insist on being number one. Be gracious. At best, you are first among equals. Good managers recognize good managers among employees. They know who is good and who has the right stuff. Give each a turn.

Step Down

Don't chair every task force in sight or put your cronies in charge. Create opportunities for trying out abilities. Send workers out to sites like farm teams but give them letters of authorization and lines of credit. Multiply your number of representatives. Write down not the vertical but the horizontal chain of command so that, if you are not around and even if you are, everyone knows whom to consult or blame.

Step Aside

Establish company priorities by management sharing. Create co-leaders. Dramatize new options as essentially leadership opportunities. Identify key themes of the unit. Create the illusion that it is the company in miniature. Aspire to top roles.

If technology or e-business is a new direction, act like chief information officers. If innovation is to be a major initiative, behave like R&D. If there is an increasing need to be sensitive to customers, make visible and present a cadre of selected customers with whom to maintain relationships.

Step Away

Every decision is minimally two decisions. One is what to do. The second is how it should happen. The mistake is that the first may be so prescriptive that it steals away the many subsequent decisions of implementation.

Authoritarian managers steal. They do not allow applications and follow-up to take place without nervous micro-managing, incessant prodding, busy-bodying monitoring, and indispensable threats or rewards. Good managers step away to create the opportunities for others to find the closure of implementation. Rather than being stars on the stage, they instead become guides on the side.

It may appear that the above steps go against the grain of the basic managerial process of stepping forward or stepping up to the plate. But what is important: hitting a home run or winning the game? And sometimes that happens best by using pinch clutch hitters.

If all this involves too much negativity, then pairing it with the balanced score card (BSC) may provide the wider organizational context for perceiving its further value. In particular, BSC can not only accommodate inhibition into virtually every level and operation but also display and affirm its effective contribution to the total organization.

Benefits of Employing BSC

Clarity
Like an X-ray, it cuts through surface to essentials and offers transparency of internal operations, trade-offs, habitual behaviors, deal making, and so forth. Every process becomes highly visible and open to inspection, review, and reformulation.

Simplicity
BSC serves as a single summary of four main complex operations. Aggregated into one main frame, BSC is also portable and can be carried by managers from one operation to another.

Consensus
BSC compels shared understanding of vision and mission but also identifies, sometimes for the first time, areas of disagreement, divergence, and difference of point of view and philosophy, especially because of unarticulated assumptions. It compels commonality of

definitions. For example, twenty-five executives agreed that superior service and targeted customers were excellent objectives. But when pressed by the score card to define what they meant by each objective, there were twenty-five different definitions.

Measurement and Management

BSC forces an alliance between the management of measurement and the measurement of management. All managers have to develop their own divisional and appropriate list of critical indicators of performance. It is not provided unilaterally from on high. In the process, managers operationalize and translate the vision and mission into divisional processes, now subject to appropriate measurements. At the same time, managers can use the same approach to test the goals and projections of the strategic business plan.

Multiple Linkages

Balanced score card always employs multiple perspectives (customers, financial, etc.), multiple measures, and multiple managerial approaches, which, in turn, generates multiple alignments of vision and mission, senior- and middle-level managers, managers and employees, and the present and the future.

Rationale for Using BSC as the Primary Mode of Assessment

Big Picture

BSC replicates the total business in miniature. At a single glance, all the essential parts can be framed and summarized. That in turn provides the focal point for discussion and definition of integration. It also accommodates new initiatives but prevents them from being favored or pet projects by insisting from the outset that they fit in and support the big picture with everything else.

Multiple Measures

No single measure can sum up the whole. Multiple measures constitute a check and balance system. Multiple measures compel interaction, integration, and consensus.

Harmonizer

BSC brings together under one roof all that is going on: customer focus, shortening response time, improving quality, reducing launch time, cutting costs, teamwork, and so forth. It corrals all initiatives in a one-stop shopping mode to determine to what degree they reinforce or oppose each other. It compels recognition of and interaction between disparate parts of the business, many of which do not ordinarily dialogue with each other. Harmony positioning requires short-term goals to be supportive, stepping stones to long-term strategies and vice versa, and forcing long-term strategies to check and, if necessary, correct the positioning of short-term steps to reach the long term.

Reallocation Decisions

Putting everything together in one big picture frame does not obscure separate, still shots of individual divisions and individuals. If financial measures only are used to add up results, then often divisions that are doing well are lumped with divisions that are not. The result is an averaging process that is distortive or lopsided. But if each division is evaluated as an independent profit center, then performance and market share determine allocation of resources. Above all, BSC alerts senior- and middle-level management to suboptimization by any one unit at the expense of another.

Alignments/Linkages

The compilation of BSC cannot be accomplished by any one person or group. It is a collective effort. In the process it aligns managers with each other: it thus helps to foster a culture of consensus and commonality of vision and goals.

Strategy Driven

BSC puts strategy, not control, in the driver's seat. The problem with using financial measures exclusively is that such measures are primarily limiting and controlling. For the short term that is acceptable, but control is not possible long term. Control also tends to pit divisions and teams against each other in unbridled competition for resources and recognition, and thus inhibits or deflects away from the creation of a consensual and cooperative environment.

Fusion of Management and Measurement

BSC is both a measurement and a management system. In fact, it manages through measurement. The process is both gradual and localized. The goals and measurements to achieve those goals are developed in tandem.

Future Driven

Unlike the focus of financial measures, BSC, especially because of the separate emphasis on innovation and creativity, is involved in future considerations. In fact, BSC is in many ways a strategic business plan, except that it is more dynamic—a performance business plan.

Questioning Culture

BSC inculcates a questioning form of inquiry. In addition, the questions stem from the perceptions of others so that managers are forced to think in terms of company performance and image rather than in personal achievement. The four main questions address the four main areas of customer, income, strategy, and innovation.

Adaptability

BSC is a form not a prescribed content. It can be adjusted to virtually every organization and sector. Indeed, it would be more accurate to claim that there are as many different BSCs and forms of inhibitions as there are companies, as many transactional consultants have discovered.

The Transactional Consultant   **19**

T HE FICTITIOUS MEMO SHOWN below was created to provide a rare and candid glimpse of how consultants often are perceived by those who hire them.

Memo to: Vice Presidents

Memo from: CEO

Subject: The Presumptive Expertise of Consultants

Who is qualified to pursue the Holy Grail of grandiose corporate solutions? Many would volunteer but there is perhaps only one group that has the necessary qualifications. They are smart, savvy, experienced, and privately at least arrogant enough to believe they know all the answers. They are regularly called upon to pull rabbits out of hats, turn employees around, and serve as confidants to CEOs.

Although it may be doubtful that they could also effectively run the companies they fix, they easily match and in some cases exceed the competence and chutzpah of most business leaders. Finally, they must be able to disappear, not take credit for turnaround, and be unremembered. The one I have retained will be onboard next week. Please extend every courtesy to her and respond to all requests for information no matter how sensitive or classified.

The consultant also asked that the following be addressed: What are the major flaws and limits of today's and our typical corporation? What are the major discords between executives, middle managers, and rank and file? Finally, what new glue and configurations are needed to face a global future?

Jumping ahead, our magician arrives and within a day or two sets herself apart from the academic experts and ex-CEOs. Professors typically hem and haw, insist on spending the bulk of their time establishing the incredible complexity of the subject, and then proceed to examine a small piece to death and pass off the fragment as whole. CEOs remain on Mount Olympus, traffic in generalities, and conclude by trotting out the old verities of hard work and loyalty. In contrast, consultants roll up their sleeves, warm to the challenge, ask immediately for all sorts of information and data, are omnipresent as their way of approaching 360, and constantly pay attention to what typically falls between the cracks. The pursuit of lost income and productivity across the board defines the difference and obsession of our integrated consultant.

In addition, what elevates consultants over all the other pretenders to the throne is that they alone possess at least five characteristics that collectively set them apart as unique and creative problem-solving convergers:

1. Fit and Access to Appearance versus Reality
2. The Detective Instinct
3. Miniature of the Whole
4. The Politics of the Cure
5. The Dynamics and Timetable of Change

Fit and Access to Appearance versus Reality

Consultants are the only outsiders allowed inside the sacred temple. They quickly discern the differences between appearance and reality, public relations and the truth. In the process, they rapidly can estimate capacity, especially of those at the top and a selected number of middle-level managers.

They are thus in a key position to undertake two interrelated assessments: Does the organization have the horses to make its proposed plan work? If not, who needs to be replaced or newly hired? HR rapidly becomes a target and the message conveyed to the CEO is that many opportunities have been lost to grow and diversify the company. It all should go back to the original basis of the hire: "Why should we hire you and your group?"

Alas, how many times have consultants been asked that daunting question from prospective clients? And it usually occurs infuriatingly after you may have already presented your strongest suit. The first bit of advice is to assume that question will be asked and thus do not shoot your bolt prematurely. If not asked, you should ask it. What are the best answers? Whatever they are, let us start off with the worst answers.

1. We are the best in the business.
2. We will save you money.
3. Given the gains, we are not that expensive.
4. We are unobtrusive and minimally invasive.
5. We do not pad the daily billables, fly first class, or eat steak every night.

Although these claims may have some truth to them, they are self-centered, whereas in truth your responses always should be client centered.

1. In many ways you and your business are unique. You are one of kind. We do not use a cookie-cutter approach. The design would be individually tailored.
2. Your company has a special future. No matter what problem we may be asked to study and solve, we are future driven. We always will provide you with a future reading of where you are going, what the major market trends are, and whether there is alignment.
3. We know you. We never take on a new client without undertaking extensive research. We know all your strengths and some of your weaknesses. We would blend in and easily be part of the operation. We would appear as insiders.
4. We measure what you are with who we are and what you manifest with what we have to offer. If there was not a match, we would not be here. We believe in making a fit.
5. But do not take our word for it. Hear what others have had to say from businesses very much like yours. Listen to this brief tape.

The Detective Instinct

Consultants are a suspicious lot. They seldom accept at face value what they are told. They don't openly deny that information. They keep their own counsel and reserve judgment. But because all consultants operate like detectives, and because they all talk endlessly to employees, three developments usually surface.

First, the trail they follow is usually interconnected and provides access to a significant cross-section of the company. The interplay between parts betrays any divisional opacity, separatism, or fragmentation Second, the inquiry process usually leads them quickly to the tentative conclusion that neither the problem nor the solution is obvious or proximate. The search then becomes a quest for the root cause, although be aware that their billable clock is always ticking.

Third, conversations with employees frequently identify the ghosts in the closet, minefields, and every once in awhile the solution to the problem. Sadly, employees are either never asked or are the last ones to be consulted even though most of the time they have the answers. (For example, professors and executives would probably never waste their time talking, let alone listening, to them.)

Miniature of the Whole

Most consultant groups directly or through associates possess 360-degree expertise. Theoretically, the business department of a university could also generate a miniature of the whole. The problem is that they are usually a collection of lone rangers determined to advance their own hobby horses and to insist on the primacy of their specialization as the only or true fount for the solution to the problem. Consultants generally are not like that. They have egos, but they usually are subdued in favor of the needs of the client. Indeed, because serving the client is paramount, the range of expertise is marshaled and brought to bear collectively on what they all are being paid for. Besides, their financial interdependence compels interdisciplinary cooperation.

The Politics of the Cure

Most problems have many solutions. They can be ranged in terms of costs, extent, personnel, and so forth. But in all cases what is always weighed by consultants is the politics of what is possible. Because they are inside the company, have spent considerable time there, talked confidentially to employees, and so on, they have developed a sense of the company's culture. They also know what each constituency wants to hear and what it does not want to hear. They also are aware of the extent to which blame and even scapegoating are waiting in the wings. What do they do? They shrewdly offer not an optimum choice but a range of possible roads to take. Here is where we have to be particularly careful.

We all exist in the same political culture. But consultants eventually leave. We are still around. We have to carefully practice the art of navigation. Two extremes have to be avoided. One involves protecting the CEO or senior management from the perception that the emperor has no clothes. The other is coming up with a respectable solution to the problem that justifies the cost, time, and dislocation of consultants.

The consultants have to be persuaded to identify, and to steer a middle course between, the clashing rocks. It is like the doctor who says to the nurse, "You give the kid the injection. I don't want him to associate pain with me."

The Dynamics and Timetable of Change

Because consultants usually have considerable experience working with many different clients in many different industries, they have acquired a comprehensive sense of what drives change; how urgent is the need (survival or growth); who opposes it; what training will be needed; what should be done first, second, and so on within what time frame; and so forth. In other words, identifying the way to go may not be enough. Every solution may have to be viewed as also a problem of the implementation and communication of the solution. Of the various alternative routes, which one is the best way to make it happen? And then how do we explain to everyone not only what the solution is but also why this route was selected above all others? If not done sensitively, tactically, and proactively, the solution can become a bigger problem than the original one it purports to solve.

In the process, consultants often are asked to stay the course and, if necessary, to clean up the mess left by change. We do not want to do that. We especially do not want to be around or occupy center stage when the play flops and the audience begins to throw things. Remember that financial interests drive consultants. They are hired, not employed. They have much in common with mercenaries, hired guns and assassins, and secret agents. They are supreme professionals working outside of the box and have to deliver the goods. They do not enjoy the security, salary, and benefits of professors or executives. They do not have a home base to come back to regularly and reassuringly. They are journeymen. They are temporary. They are scaffolding.

Although well paid for their brains, hearts, and passions, we have to make sure that, when they finish, they leave and are not remembered or missed. We have to erase and replace their nomenclature with our own. Ditto all their acronyms. If they inspired any disciples, hopefully over time they will experience some memory loss. We have to shift loyalty and admiration away from them and back to us. In less than three months, all should be sealed, cleansed, and seamless as if they have never been. All eyes should remain on us. All things should appear as if we never had any of the problems that required outside intervention. Consultants who are savvy understand that need and are not unhappy to fade into the background. Those who don't should not be invited back.

Some creatively fade into the future.

Future Leaders: New CEOs and Agendas

20

THE ANTICIPATOR

AS EVERYTHING BECOMES ROUTINELY crazy, big, and new, and relentlessly frequent and sudden, simplistic solutions, such as are usually the province of politics, are acquiring currency. In particular, there is the rallying cry for new leaders and leadership, even though that call moves in a number of contrary directions at the same time.

The new leader, given turbulent times and permissive values, needs to be a solid, sober, and stern savior. Alas, salvation reopens the door to charisma, which in the past often has led us down the garden path. The leader also should not be a celebrity or superhero anymore. Instead, the CEO should exhibit execution, humility, and, above all, post-Enron integrity. He should be almost ordinary. Finally, he could be a she or perhaps even foreign born.

The problem with all of the above is not that they are mistaken or wrong-headed but that they are piecemeal. They thus totally underestimate the range and scope of the change needed. If the total complexity of new and future CEOs is to be addressed it must be recognized that the rationale for new leaders be holistically part of a total realignment of all positions and roles. The definition of the new CEO cannot be isolated from the general dynamics of the emerging employee-manager and the manager-leader, on the one hand, or ignore the specific and different challenges of the twenty-first century, on the other hand. Here then is a composite of ten descriptors of the new leader.

Staying Power

The focus has shifted from getting the job to keeping it. In 2001 25 percent of CEOs were fired. In 2002, that went up to nearly 40 percent. The dilemma is that leaders are dammed if they do and dammed if they don't. Being a time-server and playing it safe and close to the vest won't answer the call for major changes; making excessive change and taking risk rocks the boat. Above all, CEOs who stay the course often lead companies that last. Chief executives may need to have workout gyms built next to their offices to follow the Schwarzenegger training model.

Results Driven

The job itself is now intensely and constantly measured. Personality and morale-building play second fiddle to bottom-line deliverables. Executive performance will be data managed and calculated. The new CEO may have to have an IT or project management background to be knowledgeable about information management and assessment systems, in general, and know enough to have some say about how he is being evaluated, in particular.

Process Decision-Making

Knowing whether it is working, why, and how well, and who is in charge becomes process critical. Tracking systems increasingly using real and just-in-time information resemble internally observable medical procedures that are process invasive. Data embedding has brought new access and transparency to the dynamics of customer preferences, market fluctuations, product inventory, warehouse storage capacity, and so on—all while they are going on, not after the fact. Just as express mail providers can track and tell where a package is en route, so CEOs must constantly make critical and data-driven decisions and mid-course corrections daily, even hourly. The new CEO thus may have come up from the ranks of UPS or FedEx or at least served as an airline traffic controller.

Restructuring the Organizational Chart

The new leader must fuse vision and organization. He must come to value structure and to understand how much it shapes current and future performance. Above all, he must be an internal "liberator," freeing the workplace from oppressive bosses and constraining environments. In the process, he must make first the traditional last line of all job descriptions: "Do whatever it takes." A strong background in HR will be indispensable.

Learning Leader

The call for creating a learning organization has been pushed further and harder to become the design and development of learning management systems. LMS are increasingly delivered electronically, managed cost-effectively, and implementation evaluated and affirmed.

The new leader has to develop a vision of the workforce of the future and become a tireless advocate of the training needed to get from here to there. CEO candidates unexpectedly may currently be the CIOs of corporate universities or the CLOs of learning-driven companies.

Diagnostically Driven Empowerment and Training

Knowledge of employees across the board (including at the executive level) is approaching a science. Through brain research and extensive employee testing, it is now possible to develop precise individual and group profiles of preferred performance and learning modes. With the overlay of Gardner's multiple intelligences to learning styles, the focus has shifted from "How smart am I?" to "How am I smart?" The new CEO may or may not have majored in psychology but he has to be knowledgeable about the emerging field of cognitive science.

Acknowledging and Working with a Transformed Workforce

The new CEO cannot assume a business-as-usual attitude and expect leadership deference all along the chain of command. Even the traditional sanctuary of the executive team as already noted has been pierced and reconfigured. But most important, the CEO must not only recognize but also support the emergence of manager-leaders and employee-managers. He may chafe at such leadership sharing, but if he seeks to lead a successful company, he may have to recognize and strengthen the sources of success.

Innovation

Innovation will accompany and accelerate transition. Incremental improvements of current in-house products and services will parallel and sometimes compete for resources to support achieving big, breakthrough innovations. If the forecasters are correct, innovation increasingly will be the offspring of convergence. Current fusions like bio-sociology, genetic psychology, human-machine symbiotics, and so on are but the tip of the iceberg. And the speed with which such hybrids will appear will be dizzying. It is estimated that the second decade of this century will exhibit a degree of progress ten times that of the entire twentieth century. The new CEO should be an avid reader of science fiction and require his executive team to follow suit. Ideally, he should hold a few patents.

Globality

The new CEO must be a globalist not as an occasional but as a constant focus. He must map and display an international and interoperable electronic and marketing network of suppliers, sales representatives, and customers. Overseas volatility must be added to risk management. Money managers should carefully track offshore cash flow for fluctuations against the dollar. Multinational companies may even have to shift their currency base to maintain balance. The new CEO may come from international banking and electronic commerce. He may be Chinese with an American MBA.

The Future of the Future

Of all competencies, foresight tops the list. It has to. It alone encompasses the future-driven strategies for all the above: staying power, results-driven performance, process decision-making, restructuring, learning empowerment, surviving transitions, championing innovation, and internationalism. Of all the fusions, the most critical is that between futurity and globality, which need to be paired into a seamless partnership. The new CEO will have to be a futurist and a member of the World Future Society.

In summary then, there are three common denominators that emerge as to why new CEOs may be needed, where they are likely to come from, and how they view differently globality and futurity training. Such an integrated focus raises the prospect that future CEOs should be addressing the following future agenda.

Fusion of Vision and Role

Future CEOs should be performance driven and not personality oriented; shape and put in place structures informed and guided by globality and futurity; and finally ensure that all the changes are wired in place and are so embedded that they permeate the entire organization even to the lowest rung. In addition, the future CEO must be centered on results and not cronyism or nostalgia. He must be obsessed by data measurement and statistical profiles. But now the data must exist in real and just-in-time form so as to access and render transparent the immediate flow of customer transactions, market fluctuations, inventory space, and so forth.

Transparent Communications

He must craft explanations of what is being measured, why, and how. He also has to display a global matrix along a future timeline so that every employee at every level knows that is the new way the world operates. Employees should be invited genuinely to suggest what else should be measured differently.

CEO Monthly Report Card

The CEO has to articulate performance targets (by which he is measured as well). The rallying cry is the last line of all job descriptions— "whatever it takes." Throughout, globality and futurity will become increasingly versions, and not alternatives, of each other.

Agile Structures

Perhaps the most daunting task is to find or create the right agile structures at the top and customize the expertise to meet urgent and shifting global and future challenges. There is an overall need to develop a structure that is both holistic and expert. In other words, it must miniaturize and represent the whole organization and its input, on the one hand, and be able to bring to bear quickly and precisely the expertise needed for immediate decision-making, on the other hand. The first establishes representative balance; it is democracy in miniature. The second is rotational and precludes the fixed rigidity of a Maginot line; it is a meritocracy.

Executive Conversations

The CEO needs to talk in more stirring terms without falling back on the rhetoric of charisma. Driven by the fusion of globality and futurity, the CEO has to put forth a vision over time that brings together a new big picture and features the inter-relationships of values, innovation, and learning.

Vision unfortunately has attracted more romantic heat than analytical light and has excessively set CEOs apart as lonely inhabitors of mountaintops. Nothing has wrecked more companies and resulted in more executive terminations than the inability to anticipate both the near and long-term future. And nothing has been more misguided than elevating gut instinct to the level of infallibility.

Forecasting and Trending Is Hard Work

Business intelligence gathering is not unlike the database assembled by the CIA and FBI. There are professional futurists with degrees in future studies and futurist consultants who have developed impressive strategies and scenarios for diverse companies. There have even been resident futurists in the past. Ian Wilson held such a position at General Electric for many years. In short, the vision needed by the CEO is to add to the executive team a CAO—a chief anticipatory officer—or to add that dimension to his own and to the job descriptions of all executives. Although it need not be someone brought in from the outside, it probably should not be a retread from within. The expertise of foresight is too critical to be entrusted to time servers.

Valuing and Visioning

The future direction is always to save jobs and make company goals compatible with saving jobs. That may seem obvious but layoffs and downsizing indicate otherwise. In fact, many CEOs basically have chosen fast and dirty solutions: save companies by eliminating jobs. They have not learned the lesson of Henry Ford, who paid his workers more than others so they could afford to buy his cars. National policy has to become corporate policy. Wherever possible, employment and company survival have to be joined at the hip; CEOs have to agonize rather than amputate.

Wedding Anticipatory Management with Participatory Management

CEOs need to set up company-wide input on future directions. Every employee at every level has to be reshuffled into cross-divisional teams and during brown bag breakfasts or lunches become involved in studying the future. To keep the process anchored and to forestall blue-skying, the focus should initially be on the future of their job and expertise. Scenarios need to be written of what that job will be like two to five years from now and, if considerably different, what it will take to get from here to there.

Future-Driven Workforce

Aside from generating and contributing grassroots perceptions of the future, the fusion of anticipation with participation will help to shape a workforce that is minimally future oriented and optimally future driven. There is no point in projecting a future if the means to get there are not made available. Employee identification of the supplemental skills they will need in the future not only makes them more receptive to change and growth but also defines the company's training agenda. Futurizing also can lead to innovation.

Innovation Creates the Future

The new moves us beyond the now to the then and the there. Indeed, it can be further claimed that one of the most stimulating ways of stirring innovation across the board is to make all employees futurists. But like the figure of Janus, which faces back and forward at the same time, innovation must be applied in both directions. Current products or services already in-house need to be tinkered with, reconfigured to require fewer steps, and moved more rapidly across divisional lines—in short, incrementally improved. Such day-to-day improvements are small but cumulative; they add up.

As far as technological breakthroughs from the outside, that is often a wild card. Often unknown and unexpected, some are nevertheless discoverable. Futurists have been able to anticipate two-thirds of future technology, but they also have missed the other one-third. Science fictionists may have a better track record. Companies need to maintain or outsource advance guards to monitor the edge for coming attractions. But even then the feasibility and durability of each new imminent development requires the use of an evaluative tool, such as the expert Delphi. Collaborative synergy is at the heart of the innovative spirit and its nature and intensity constantly has to reflect the learning curve of its collective experts if it is to exceed the present.

Finally, the CEO needs to project a vision that not only aligns globality with foresight, but also embodies the values, innovation, and learning both will require. Finally, that symbiotic fusion of vision and role not only is generated by, but also applies to and serves to evaluate, CEO performance.

This workforce is genuinely new and transformational. Nothing quite like it has ever existed before. It has been shaped and evolved by the convergence of globality and futurity. The CEO thus has to resist the temptation to reverse such growth by going back in time to create obedient, narrowly defined jobs suitable for overseas outsourcing. This genuinely brilliant American achievement must not be undone or trivialized to meet short-term and small bottom-line gains. In the long run—and that has to be the vision of the CEO—this workforce will sustain and restore American preeminence in the workplace here and globally.

In the process, it might be helpful also for CEOs to explore the history and role of the prophets.

Ancient Prophets and Modern Forecasters

THE WORD "PROPHET" IS DERIVED FROM the Greek word *prophetes*, which means "one who speaks forth." The Greek translators of the Bible used that term to designate the *hozeh* (visionary) and *ro'eh* (seer). But the most common Hebrew title is *navi* (man) or *neviah* (woman), which means appointed messenger of God charged with communicating God's will to the people.

The concept of the *navi* ended with the canonization or official acceptance of the parts of the Hebrew bible in the fifth century BCE. Later Jewish rabbinic tradition declared in the Talmud that prophecy had come to an end. But a number of other rabbis, including Maimonides himself, argued that prophecy was ongoing and would reappear whenever God willed it or found an appropriate candidate for His message. In fact, Rabbi Michael Shire published a book in 2001 titled *The Jewish Prophet*, which tied the prophetic tradition from Moses and Miriam to Theodore Herzl and David Ben-Gurion.

Rabbi Shire divides the history of the Jewish prophets into three periods. The first is biblical and post-biblical and ranges from Moses to Rabbis Hillel and Akiva. The second period covers the Middle Ages and comes up to modern times. It ranges from Maimonides to the Bal Shem Tov, the founder of Hasidism. Finally, the twentieth century includes Martin Buber, Abraham Heschel, and (as noted) Herzl and Ben-Gurion.

Such a claim of Jewish prophecy across the ages requires that we be able to define what makes a prophet a prophet if for no other reason than to distinguish the true from false prophets. Then, too, the definition must be encompassing—include the biblical, as well as the modern. So what can be said are some of the common distinguishing characteristics of Jewish prophets?

1. Intensity, often approaching ecstasy. Urgent, almost obsessive in his or her singular focus. Single minded, with an agenda.
2. Explicitly linked with God. Speaks to and for Him. Abraham Heschel also calls the prophet a partner or associate with God. Divinely inspired, stirred, and guided.
3. Enunciates and defines a divine plan. Life and history are not haphazard, unmoldable, or unchangeable. All is purposeful.
4. Corrective. Things need to change. Each of us needs to change our ways to be in accord of what God requires of us.
5. Embedded in Jewish tradition and values, especially those of the biblical prophets. Establish Jewish continuity and the heritage of the covenants.
6. Focus on this world, not the afterlife, and on reaching the promised land by improving, healing, and fixing the world so that it is worthy of our being created in the image of God. Judaism shall be a light unto the nations by means of actions.
7. Futuristic visions warning of dire consequences that may come or upholding a vision of a more spiritual, rich, and harmonious world in which the lion shall lie down with the lamb, and swords will be beaten into plowshares.

Of course, like Rabbi Shire, if figures like Theodor Herzl and David Ben-Gurion are to be counted as Jewish prophets, at least two adjustments are necessary. First, we have to accept Jewish history, in addition to biblical times, as having validity. Second, they have to be designated as secular prophets to relieve them of the burden of being inspired by God. With those two criteria applied, we can turn rapidly to and assess contemporary prophets.

Forecasting appears to be steadily maturing. Singular bases have been replaced wisely by mixed-mode forecasting. Technology projections no longer are embarrassed by being coupled with science fiction but rather enjoy a mutual synergy. Global model building is emerging in more robust forms and making significant contributions, especially to environmental futures. But one area that has not been mined as much as perhaps it should be is that of the history of ideas or rather the history of future ideas.

This is particularly critical because virtually all of the most significant forecasts of the last twenty-five years have possessed an intellectual core. Indeed, such constructs have served to link past and future preoccupations with major concepts and thus have served to strengthen the long-range point of view. One such concept that has been surfacing in diverse forms and attracts analysis is that of convergence.

Long-range planners and futurists routinely and wisely employ mixed-mode forecasting. They do not put all their eggs in one basket but combine a variety of forecasting modes or systems, sometimes intentionally at odds with one another, but generally harmonious. In fact, that has been the general practice since it was advocated by Ian Mitroff and Harold Linstone many years ago and characterized as "multiple forecasting." What, however, is less often discussed or acknowledged is why the mixture works well together.

An examination of a number of mixed-mode forecasts reveals that the forecasters consciously have selected modes that internally task and test each other. It is not just that they are different. They are also potentially antagonistic. They function as a check and balance system. It is as if the dynamics of the forecast, as well as the yields, are subject to the give and take of an internal review panel. Put together that way, the forecast appears more robust, exudes and attracts greater confidence, and is admirably displayed as an elegant proof. The forecast displays the same good muscularity because it was created in the image of its well-crafted mix of modes.

To be sure, certain mode partnerships seem to work particularly well, almost symbiotically. For example, technological forecasting does very well when it is regularly linked to science fiction. The productive antagonism between science and imagination offers a degree of comfort and surprise and a creative mixture of intelligence and ingenuity. The result is impressive "imagineering." Similarly, research forecasting often benefits from scenario or simulation, which serves not only to explain and to anchor the projected research but also to test and reflect back on the research and/or its explanation. Scenarios exploring the ramifications of human genome research would be an excellent example.

Although the admixture of modes generates, when it works well, the benefits of harmonious discord, it is probably not possible and certainly not very interesting to identify with predictable specificity all the ingredients of an optimum mixed mode. There are just too many variables of all kinds, including cultural ones.

But there may be some common denominators—some constants that most, if not all, robust forecasts seem to have. Examining a number of forecasts over the last twenty-five years, of all kinds, in all sectors, by diverse hands, one also finds that those with that internal check and balance dynamic all possess an intellectual core. That is, they are driven forward (and often connected backward) by a conceptual power that is usually big, embracing, and ultimately seminal. The content resembles that of the history of ideas, except, of course, it is projected forward.

Indeed, one of the key tests is whether the idea, in addition to its depth, has sufficient horizontal thrust to be lodged in the future and there to offer a grand outline whose ultimate shape is not totally or finally clear or visible.

In other words, ideally mixed-mode forecasting is considerably strengthened by intellectual force—by conceptual power. Perhaps, offering and examining a specific example of a future-driven idea might achieve two ends: documenting the kind of idea that helps to sustain powerful forecasting and contributing to the history of future ideas one that may dominate the twenty-first century.

It has never been easy being a futurist—persuading CEOs, presidents, companies, and workers that real and reliable data exists about what is likely to happen, when, and what its impacts will be, without claiming total certainty how such trends can guide future decisions. In addition, when it also involves telling the emperor he has no clothes, that makes it even a harder sell. Indeed, often when futurists meet at conferences, they exchange not just ideas but also martyrdoms—you show me your stigmata and I will show you mine.

But just when futurists have become accustomed to accepting the recurrent historical challenge of being messengers of disconnect and accordingly sometimes shot, they are increasingly being informed that they in turn need to change—that they are part of a first generation of futurists, and that what is being called for now is a second generation of forecasters. But what invests this passing of the baton with particular importance is its potential for wider insight and even paradigm shifts.

Somehow the study of the future has deep and interconnected roots—so much so that when the parameters of futurism are altered that generally signals wider reverberations across the board. In other words, presumption rules: as we identify some of the new factors that now seem to be characteristic of a second generation of futurists, we should be aware that we may also be describing a second generation of companies, universities, and even countries.

It is probably not accidental that so many of our seminal futurists are now older and serve as senior statesmen. Forecasters like Joseph Coates, Ed Cornish, Arnold Brown, Clement Bezold (who sadly just died), and many others here and abroad epitomize a generation of independent and often feisty originals who in many ways established and bequeathed the standards of the profession that are still operative today. But no matter how many associates they would call upon to join or amplify them, they all were singular geniuses—opinionated lone rangers always telling it as it is—always worth listening to and learning from. What extended the range of their singularity was their extensive and broad-based set of clients who sought multiple applications and solutions. In other words, who they were as futurists was shaped and extended by who they served. Although not multiple by training, their diverse masters compelled 360-degree thinking. But the one steadying and consistent piece was the absolute transferability of their evolving methodologies.

The second generation of futurists, of course, stands on the broad shoulders of such giants in many respects. The most obvious mantle they have to adopt and adapt is that of being multiperspectival. But now modality is trickier, hidden, even ubiquitous—not so much chosen as compelled by the incredibly complex interconnectivity of globality as a new norm of forecasting.

What we find now is that every local or regional client is global; every US employee has an international counterpart working beside him; boutiques in the aggregate equal a major competitor. The principal issue that emerges for this second generation of futurists is how to understand and manage the unprecedented simultaneity of global diversity.

Being multidisciplinary may not be enough. We need to be interdisciplinary—so that the complexity of that known and unknown interconnectivity will be at least a match for that of the world, ideally with the two essentially becoming versions of each other. But how is that to be accomplished? Minimally, there are at least three ways of fusing globality and interdisciplinarity: the short term, or restructuring what we do now; an intermediate mid-term of reframing direction; and the long term of developing systems of systems. Although the timetable and content of all three developments could be hastened if the academy as a whole could shift its focus from specialization to interdisciplinary training, glaciers are unlikely to move rapidly or make such radical shifts. The training programs of some international businesses could make such shift, if they made unlearning a staple of turnaround. But in the meantime, we have to work with what we have and do so as creatively and futuristically as we can.

The basic building block now and increasingly in the future is the team. Every time we create a task force that brings together a number of different disciplines, we are simulating a range of perspectives that exceeds that of the individual members of the team. In such a case it would not be an exaggeration to claim that the whole is greater than its parts. (Of course, we don't know what we would say if all the participants were already multidisciplinary.)

But to fully engage and simulate global complexity the problem-solving capacity of such teams in turn requires, as noted above, at least three kinds of futuristic restructuring. The first involves becoming more holistic; the second requires occupying intersects and being focused on innovation; and the third invites the dazzling prospect of global systemics.

The Holistic

A new car battery was being developed for an all-electric car. To test it, a team of engineers was assembled, each one representing a different car function. Each acted autonomously. Their expertise ranged from ignition, spark plugs, lights, air conditioning, radio, and so forth. When the total specs determined by each function were loaded in and became operational, the battery failed—the demand was greater than the supply. The typical solution was to berate the experts on their excesses and then by trial and error make the necessary adjustments. Instead, all of them were asked to play the role of the battery and apportion what was needed without draining the battery dry. With each one becoming the custodian of the battery's integrity, balanced output was achieved. Collective needs replaced competitive and separate demands, and holistic group problem solving produced a win–win situation.

In this case study, ultimate success was predicated on identifying the major core and then fusing all outputs and inputs until they became one or more versions of each other. Thinking and acting collectively and holistically in turn requires future futurists increasingly to move from the circumference to the center and to find and fix the micro in the macro. In short, positioning is everything.

The Innovative Intersect

Frans Johansson makes a critical distinction in *The Medici Effect* (2006) between directional and intersectional ideas. The former are known, generally predictable, and incremental. They are all the new improvements—of all things, all operating systems, all operations, all communications. Every company does it 24/7. Everyone seeks to build a better mousetrap, eliminate expensive steps on the production line, reduce the weight of an airplane, and so forth.

Such adjustments and tweaking go on all the time and find expression in cost reduction and higher levels of productivity and profitability. Even the non-crass area of mathematics is unidirectional: a five-stage proof rendered in four is dubbed an elegant proof. The entire effort is driven by the impossible dream of perfection and the constant and incremental pursuit of that ideal—until someday a perfect mousetrap will be built.

Then one day someone discovers a way to eliminate mice altogether without having to use a mousetrap at all. The standard way is bypassed. Suddenly, without warning and (as it were) from out of left field, comes a solution; only now it is not called new but innovative or, in Johansson's terms, an intersectional idea. Such ideas are different, perhaps even unique, in at least three ways: direction, knowledge range, and outputs.

Unlike directional ideas, which obediently can go in only one direction—that of improvement—intersectional ideas occupy a central position at a crossroads and thus can go unpredictably in as many directions as there are points on a compass. They can even pursue many directions at the same time. Intersectional ideas are thus like the future itself—an unpredictable and unfinished cornucopia.

Similarly, intersection by definition is not so much a given body of knowledge as a range of knowledge existing at the points of intersect where various disciplines meet or can be persuaded to talk, to converge, to problem solve. The intersect is thus a movable feast. It is not known in advance but evolves. It is not a fixed point, but in fact is created by the dialogue of interdisciplinarity. And, above all, it is temporary or tentative in that it serves as scaffolding to support the prospect of new relationships and conversations.

Finally, it generates unique outputs, which include opening up entirely new fields of study and production; developing supporters, followers, and advocates; creating not just ways of doing business but also new businesses; and changing the world. Perhaps then it is not surprising that every intersect is a rehearsal for the future because every innovation creates the future.

System of Systems

The new generation of futurists must become advocates—and help to construct the major challenge of the twenty-first century: composite models of all systems on the order and magnitude of the human genome project. It would not be a separative but interactive system involving all factors and drivers: human and animal demographics, socioeconomic, geophysical, ecological—in short, the works. It also would have to incorporate, or serve as an overlay for, a number of new evolving partnerships and multidirectional choices.

The most obvious is the new or rediscovered relationship of coexistence of the human and the natural—the aspiring dynamics of Abraham Maslow contending with environmental conservation. To those primal forces would be added the heady complication of human transformation or amplification as the symbiosis of artificial intelligence and its clever mechanics and electronics takes hold.

A new addition or corrective of simplexity may have to become part of the equation. Future solutions may have to be more inspired by biological functionality than mechanical perfection. Simple and inexpensive solutions like peanut butter–based food for starving babies, a hole in the ground to improve sanitation, and jets that don't go any faster but operate more efficiently may help save the day and the future.

Although other dimensions surely could be added, the key question is whether such a system of systems can be compiled and, if so, what it would do for us. Both issues partly were answered imperfectly a number of years ago in the construction of a global model by Meadows and Forrester and described in their book *The Limits to Growth*. Of course, the model was seriously but instructively flawed, especially in its failure to appreciate the mischief of certain variables that inconsiderately leaked on other variables. But that can be fixed in future versions or, if not, at least allowed for. In other words, it is doable.

But there were two additional reverberating values to this pioneering effort. The first was unexpected and therefore critical. Many misread the title and took the limits to growth to mean the end of growth; so powerful and fearful is the prospect of developmental promise that clearly it has to be factored into any new global model of models. But flawed and misinterpreted though it was, its authors came up with a final conclusion that perhaps redeemed the entire venture: namely, there is no human goal that requires more people to achieve it. Of course, that statement also added to the firestorm, but perhaps that should be the measure of their—and our—project: that it disturbed the world.

Hopefully, our future futurists in the process of repositioning and occupying the center, existing at the multiple edges of the intersect, and finally building the system of systems similarly will bring us the gifts of greater clarity and hope as the legacy of a new generation. But they also have to apply the future to everyday realities without denying its mystery.

Future-Driven Leadership Applications **22**

NOTHING IS EVER FINISHED OR done once and for all time. Nor is even being current enough. What's new inevitably has to involve what's next. The future is no longer respectful of time barriers but crosses over at will, invades the present, and establishes transition as the new operating norm. But again what is amazing is the workforce's adaptability, its doing whatever it takes to catch up, keep up, and get ahead. That in fact is the often untold and unexamined story of not only the new twenty-first century American work ethic but also why the United States will remain a future global force.

In addition, there are at least five other major future-driven applications that already are operational: new training metrics; new strategic planning modes; corporate universities and their knowledge cultures; employee empowerment and productivity; and the future learning leaders—CLOs.

New Training Metrics
How have organizations and individuals coped with flux? Basically through three kinds of training and learning: catch-up, line-up, and cross-over.

Catch-Up
The thrust of catch-up is incremental: bringing professionals up to date with the latest developments. These are usually add-ons.

Occasionally, they may incorporate new directions but in almost all cases they are focused and designed to bring everyone to the cutting edge or state of the art. Although future influenced, they are essentially present bound.

Line-Up
Line-up is about structure not content. It is multidirectional and requires not so much the acquisition of new knowledge or skills as their constant repositioning and prioritizing. The aim is to align individual and divisional goals with company objectives, especially if there are satellite centers, and especially if these are multinational. A key new learning complexity is managing and aligning multicultural and multigenerational diversity and values.

Cross-Over
Cross-over involves two kinds of additional learning. One is cross-training. Co-workers are trained in each others' jobs for replacement purposes, if necessary, and, more importantly, to expand the knowledge and skills base of workers.

The other cross-over is more structurally ambitious—more interoperable. It involves linking the work focus of different divisions with each other to promote greater collaboration. It may link such operations as planning and customer service, marketing and auditing, purchasing and production, and so forth. Employees may spend a day or week for example on the phone in customer service. The goal is greater integration of function and process across the board.

New Strategic Planning Modes
Because of increasing uncertainty and discontinuity, strategic forecasting needs futures thinking if it is to preserve its integrity as a discipline, on the one hand, and sustain the reality of its mid- and long-term projections, on the other. The changes required reflect the degree to which the knowledge of at least three distinctive ways the future operates has been incorporated into strategic planning methodologies: in particular, patterns of escalation, degrees of knowability, and the partnership of monitoring.

Responding to future discontinuity varies over reaction time and with advanced intelligence. In fact, the goal of strategic planning is to preserve decision time and options. But that in turn requires perceiving unfolding developments in the progressive and aggressive terms of stretch, strain, and shock. The sequence is ruled by a law of grim escalation. The first version of stretch, if ignored, is followed by the second; if that in turn elicits no response, then the third dominates the scene.

If the future is an enigma, it is often a transparent one. It is an amalgam of the known, the unknown, and the unknowable. The obvious strategy is to move the knowledge base along that continuum. Extrapolation of present data and demographics builds the extent of the known in the present and short term. Trending converts the unknown into knowable long-term patterns. But then all stops short with the unknowable because that is in fact what defines the final future. But the consolation is that as much as two-thirds can be in hand.

Monitoring is no longer occasional and external but permanently embedded. It constitutes at least half of planning. Tracking sensors are distributed throughout to function as an early warning system to catch deviations. Monitoring requires its own plan. Usually it is a permanent overlay of data tracking equipped with its own software program that has the capacity to adjust planning when certain parameters are exceeded and calculated.

The futuristic adjustments of strategic planning produce a more integrated and dynamic whole, and also—and here again is the critical point—the plan itself would be a futures thinking document. It would behave like the future.

Corporate Universities and Their Knowledge Cultures

The incredible growth of corporate universities, ranging from McDonald's to Ford to Disney to Toyota, bears witness to the centrality of training and learning as a major American and especially multinational investment in the future. Constantly responding to new challenges, corporate universities in the process have been involved minimally in two major future-oriented shifts: multinational acculturation and e-learning.

Acculturating new employees whose work cultures are different and may in fact be at variance from that of the desired mainstream is an increasing focus of global companies. For example, Dell employs a number of software programmers from India and recently outsourced a significant portion of their customer tech support there. Typically, employees from India favor supervisors who tell them what to do. They find it difficult to act on their own initiatives. They prefer description to opportunity. Dell, which values worker participation over obedience and nonlinear thinking over rote, employs extensive situational training to bring about a shift in values and thereby a shift in work dynamics.

The other major change is the gradual conversion to e-learning. In some cases, a blended approach has been used for older, less technologically comfortable workers: traditional face-to-face classes have been joined with e-classes.

The primary motivation is cost: lower instructional costs, less time away from work, elimination of travel and per diem expenses to centralized training sites, and so forth. The other gain is increased quality control through standardization of content in the three areas noted above: catch-up, line-up, and cross-over.

To a large extent, corporate universities are themselves future entities. They embody Senge's learning organization and incorporate knowledge workers, which, when combined, create unique knowledge and learning cultures. They are almost like countries in their own right. To be sure, unlike traditional academic universities, corporate universities are ideological. They promote the perpetuation of their own survival and growth, as well as the bottom line. They are their own lobbyists. They in effect use themselves as case studies.

But individually and collectively, they also need to be corporate global citizens by including the new ideologies of global interdependence and sustainable development. It is not enough to hail and benefit from the global economy. It also requires the unique leadership of multinationals calling for and aspiring to world stewardship of the global commons. Such a commitment requires going beyond singular ideology to embrace an interdependent ideology, which commands the international respect and loyalty of all professionals. In both instances, the value of futures thinking again is thus inevitably visionary.

Finally, futures thinking would encourage convergent thinking, which raises the integration of thought and process to optimum levels of synthesis without compromising differentiation. Whether or not the singularity occurs according to its projected timetable, what is clear is that it is born of and driven by convergence.

Edward Wilson called it consilience to signify the future synergistic math of one plus one equaling three or four or five. Emily Dickinson claimed that "everything that rises converges." Discoveries or breakthroughs at the apex will in volcanic fashion reach out, touch, extend, and enrich all the other apexes to produce a total greater than the sum of its parts. In short, the visionary corrective here is that the future itself is essentially a convergent force.

Employee Empowerment and Productivity

The obvious goal of training and learning is to increase the holy trinity of productivity, profitability, and quality. Of the three, the first enjoys the highest priority because of the competition of the global economy. To preserve their middle-class status, American workers have had to become more productive. Often because of downsizing, that also involves fewer workers doing more. Although there are many ways of increasing worker productivity, one approach that has received generally less attention and offers the option of a major application of futures learning and thinking is that of the employee evaluation.

In the last five years the nomenclature has changed. Employee evaluation has become performance evaluation and then shifted to its present version of performance improvement. Employees themselves have become human capital and as such training is perceived as a way of securing return on investment (ROI). Worker agreements have in many organizations become worker contracts and finally worker covenants. The common denominator of all these changes is the increasing centrality of employee productivity and the increasing dependence of companies on the capacity of workers to constantly create or find cost-savings and creative ways of increasing productivity. There are signs that some organizations are contemplating a futures step in the performance improvement process.

Currently, the standard way to improve productivity is to encourage employees to consider how they might do their jobs differently. Many managers, especially those with seniority, have had to be retrained as coaches. They found it difficult to confer such initiatives upon the workers they supervise and to grant to those who do the job the expertise that they know it better than anyone else.

In some instances, the inquiry into performance improvement has been pushed further in two ways: asking employees to define and evaluate the effectiveness of the interfaces between divisions, encouraging more overt interpersonal attitudes and behaviors so that receiving work satisfaction is accompanied by giving it as well to others. The gains have been significant. Structural changes have been made and interpersonal behavior modification has improved the mutuality of work environments. Matters appear to have gone as far as they can go, in the present.

The next logical step is to push inquiry into the future itself. Although the changes recommended by employees on doing their jobs more productively are welcome, they are still present-bound. They deal with new configurations of various kinds, but they are generally incremental in nature. But endowing empowerment with more forward-looking vistas, workers can be invited to speculate on what they believe their jobs will be like in the future. Building upon their increasing competence in job review and change, workers may not only welcome such an opportunity but also warm to the task of projecting their future roles. Such worker projections can be followed by inquiring what kinds of training would be critical to get them from here to there. Such speculation can be a gradual, rather than a one-shot, process and also may be accompanied by discussion and the distribution of some basic reading materials. In any case the yields can be significant.

Individual projections of work change can be aggregated upward to generate patterns of the future which may shape that of the company itself. In addition, the same process may identify common training needs and in effect identify the training agenda of the future. Of perhaps greater long-term importance, the process would contribute to developing a future-directed work force.

Finally, those companies supportive of such futures empowerment would have in effect created an employee-based alternative to the expert model in the form of futures learning communities. In all the above instances, the vision of the future not only brings a new dynamic to work environments but also shapes futures learning communities of best practices.

Future Learning Leaders: Chief Learning Officers

One of the signs of the future arriving ahead of schedule is the emergence of jobs and titles for which there is often no previous classification or formal academic preparation. The positions of chief information officer (CIO) and chief learning officer (CLO) are cases in point. No traditional or even corporate universities offer masters programs or degrees in learning management or have retrofitted existing executive educational programs to accommodate learning leadership at an executive level. And yet professionals are being appointed to such top-level positions, and a new journal (hardcopy and online), professional organization, and website have appeared devoted to the CLO.

For many, the appearance of CIOs and CLOs comes out of the blue. Not so for futurists, but then they may be not only reenacting the emergence of futurists themselves decades ago but also sharing their obsession with what is to come. Indeed, one can study and compile the emergence of every new profession as reflecting the regular and most current incarnation of the future. In any case, such emergence already has left its mark and permeated the entire organization, including by defining the hybrid nature of CEOs.

Table 22.1. Futures Thinking and Learning Summary Matrix

Current Focus	Futures Contribution	Future Outcomes
1. New Training Norms	Transition Training	Optimizing Knowledge
2. New Strategic Planning	Strategic Monitoring	Optimizing Choice
3. Corporate Universities	Global Interdependence	World Citizens
4. Employee Productivity	Future Work Projections	Future Workforce
5. Learning Management	Future Learning Foci	Future Intelligence

Table 22.2.   Futures Responses to Steep Learning Curves

Futures Thinking	Divergent and Convergent
Futures Problem Solving	Multiple Methodologies
Futures Learning	Multiple Intelligences
Futures Visioning	Intuitive and Holistic Forethought

Perhaps the best way to summarize HR future-driven developments and applications can be seen in table 22.1.

And similarly perhaps the best way of expressing what futures thinking at different levels can bring to the learning and HR challenges of the twenty-first century is to offer the information shown in table 22.2.

In short, the future always has the last word.

The Ideology of Convergence   **23**

THE INTEGRATOR

> *It is usual to treat Leonardo as a scientist and as a painter in separate studies. And no doubt the difficulties in following his mechanical and scientific investigations make this a prudent course. Nevertheless, it is not completely satisfactory, because in the end the history of art cannot be properly understood without some reference to the history of science. In both we are studying the symbols by which man affirms his mental scheme, and these symbols, be they pictorial or mathematical, a fable or a formula, will reflect the same changes.*
>
> —KENNETH CLARK, *LEONARDO DA VINCI* (1993)

EVERY MAJOR FORECASTING EFFORT of the last twenty-five years has exhibited an intellectual core. To the traditional history of ideas, forecasters have added the history of future ideas. The key task has always been to discover the major forces in the present driving future development. What appears to be emerging now is a resurgence of the pursuit of unified knowledge. What is there about the current situation and the next two decades that is pressuring and presaging a preoccupation with the integration and unification of all knowledge? Who are some of the major figures and what are the shaping factors which individually and collectively help to determine whether the content generated has the conceptual power to function as a mega-trend?

Three representative areas of convergent thought will be examined. The first deals with the technology and theology of convergence; the second with the socioeconomic and political dimensions of "connexity"; and the third with the "consilience" of science and the humanities. Finally, a summary of the range and substance of those three areas should serve to establish the basis for designating convergence as a mega-trend.

Convergence: Technology and Theology

According to many, "the universe of one science" exists and presupposes a constellation of common research inquiries and activities. There is always the many before there is the one. Gradually, however, discrete and scattered strands of inquiry coalesce, become initially a cluster and then a consortium of cross-fertilization, and finally converge and emerge as a powerful force with a common theoretical and intellectual agenda.

To make sense of this dynamic progression and to provide reassuring tangibility, the future is often rendered as a new creation story or science fiction focused on the specifics of creating, for example, autonomous humans, amplified and potentially ageless. And so begins the sometimes uneasy partnership between technology and theology.

Two frontiers already have been crossed. The first involves what is called the "internal pharmacy," by which humans can be maintained at an individualized optimum level automatically. A metabolic profile is developed for each individual and to it are pegged all known medications, chemicals, and nutrient supplements to maintain optimum balance. When implanted, it monitors the various functions and vital signs that are to be maintained and dispenses the appropriate chemical in the appropriate amount to maintain efficacy. All of this builds on new implant and sustained release technology of drugs or electrical charges that have been disease-specific (cancer or diabetes). As a result, there is already considerable expertise and even familiarity with the procedures.

But if this is a quantum jump, it is because it is based on a total understanding of the interacting and integrating dynamics of the entire human system. It is that convergence of knowledge that provides the intellectual base for producing a complete metabolic profile of each individual. Perhaps its greatest value, given genetic predictors and family history, is to provide proactive options to be involved in preventive medicine.

The second convergence of this magnitude is what has been called "the third intelligence." Incremental knowledge only adds to the overload. What is needed is pattern recognition of knowledge patterns and paths between and across knowledge areas. Only such models of integrated knowledge clusters can then comprehend multiple reverberating effects of drug interactions, the dynamics of global pollution and recovery, and finally thinking in ten dimensions. But this is easier said than done: How do we get there?

Our technology needs to undergo a double development. It has to be given, first, a range of sensory inputs (with enough blank space to accommodate more) and, second, the neural ability to create its own perceptions. Development along cloning lines is not the way to go. That is the incremental direction. What we need is an interfacing chip that can understand the way we think and conceive and yet possesses its own intelligence, which is intentionally different and even divergent.

It is a permeable relationship: sometimes equal, sometimes not; sometimes one dominating, sometimes the other, sometimes neither. But although the fit initially at least has to be mutual and consensual, it must be allowed to develop, on the one hand, and to call on other means when the problem exceeds the combined power and comprehension of the third intelligence, on the other hand. In short, the projected convergence requires human–technological intervention in the evolution of the species—a new Adam and Eve—with the midwife being unlimited synthesis.

But is it doable? In the human brain there is no distinction between hardware and software. The biological neural networks of the brain are instead a special kind of intelligent hardware that is not completely fixed at birth but evolves and modifies with time as the person grows and learns. In other words, part of the daunting complexity of the brain is that it is already integrated—hardware and software—whereas our current intelligent machines are dualistic. Then, too, the neural networks of the brain not only change with patterns of use and experience but also in the process they generate "the mind," which is a combined creation of the brain and information and learning. Increasingly the brain and the mind develop a master-servant relationship. In other words, it is no small matter to design "brain chips," but it is an incredibly difficult task to design "mind chips." Finally, the brain-mind is a self-programming, self-learning, and self-managing system. It is autonomous. Reconfigurable hardware, once programmed for sufficient autonomy, has about it the promise of being self-regulating, thus supportive of precisely the way the mind thinks and learning proceeds. The test of whether it is a successful mimic of the mind is whether it helps to develop information impact and causes change.

Sometimes, the applications and objects of projected convergences surface even before the theoretical and intellectual convergence knowledge base has fully solidified. One occurred after the Civil War and involved the convergence of piano and firearms technology to produce the first rudimentary typewriter. The results of convergence are greater than the sum of its parts. In the process, science increasingly will sound like religion. But that is not totally surprising. In fact, if nature were not so profound to begin with, science would not exist at all. There would be nothing to explain, no patterns to be found, and no order to be discovered. The classic comment by Einstein is correct: "The most incomprehensible thing about the universe is that it is comprehensible." Thus, science's quest for convergence is really and always a quest for the origins of all things. In this connection, the human genome is the mother lode. It offers re-creation. Much of the intellectual novelty and power of convergence is that it will finally bring about a fusion of science and religion, Prometheus and God. Indeed, the scope of current and future scientific inquiry was originally the exclusive preserve of priests and mystics. Although the issue of the origins of the laws of nature is strictly speaking not scientific but metaphysical, that separation is no longer respected or valued.

But three major objections surface. First, what have been called patterns of coming together occur all the time in nature and just as often come asunder. But to invest the occasional or even frequent patterns of convergence with the force of a total and permanent arrangement is to inflate the significance of partial occurrence with a reassurance that just is not there.

Second, man is not unique. Evolution operates not by progress but by diversity and variation and there are many species of Homo sapiens. Then, too, the complexity of human design and human society is greater than that of nature. The number of variables is so great that it cannot be understood let alone managed. Finally, the convergence really seeks to attack the last great frontier and to take on time itself. It is nothing less than the ultimate presumption of immortality.

The last issue is a real one, but the proponents of convergence are not willing at this point to contemplate anything so absolute or arrogant. In effect they are really talking about longevity or relative immortality and not an absolute condition. But what is dramatically clear is that the new technology born of convergence is in effect a theology. Indeed, the ultimate synthesis may be to make them one.

Misgivings about understanding and managing human and societal complexity is in fact a central focus of Geoff Mulgan, who directs a think tank, teaches at University College London, and was, most importantly for our focus, a member of Prime Minister Tony Blair's policy unit. The title of his book *Connexity* not only introduces a new and futuristic term to the discussion of synthesis but also takes a new direction. Mulgan's concern is with culture, especially the culture of politics, government, and social change. His contribution to and reinforcement of the theory of convergence is thus offered from a social science perspective.

To Mulgan, human history basically has been preoccupied by three major definitions of the sociopolitical self. All three currently coexist in different countries, societies, and classes because the world is a total time machine.

The first one is the culture of dependence in which freedom is in very short supply and a single dominant and dominating ideology and theology is tyrannically in place. Deservedly, maintains Mulgan, wherever that kind of bondage prevails it is appropriately designated as the "dark ages." Happily, declarations of independence, through both revolution and evolution, usher in a culture not only of democratic, egalitarian, and proactive discourse but also of unbridled and unshackled inquiry.

Indeed, it is from this emancipation that the twins of democracy and science emerged and flourished. But Mulgan finds substantial evidence for the emergence of a third or new phase: interdependence. Like the phases that preceded it, interdependence came about as an antidote to excessive freedom and to the notion of the self as sovereign. In conditions and cultures of freedom, the individual rules supreme and feels free to call upon all the means of his society to protect and even increase his freedom, especially when anything appears to challenge, contain, or abridge it.

The net result is an ambiguously liberating and self-indulgent society of free-wheeling, self-contained, autonomous individuals whose orbits are unrestrained and undirected. This is basically a win/lose process in which the self wins but social coherence loses. But what Mulgan sees emerging are individuals and societies that increasingly accept that they are connected to everyone, and everything else exists in a web of mutual interdependence evolving towards a higher integration. The alternative culture increasingly accepted and encouraged by both psychologists and sociologists is one in which the self is perceived as less of a given, less complete, less whole. Maturing means accepting your incompleteness, your permeability to other people.

Although Mulgan clearly favors this new image of the self in an increasingly interconnected society, he sees it as largely voluntary in Western cultures and more of a tradition in Eastern cultures. But he does argue rightly that it is being hastened on the one hand by need and by enlightenment on the other.

Thus, the incredible commitment in business to interdependent teams is being driven by intense competition and by the capacity of teams to be more innovative. Indeed, that "teamness" is celebrated by a new term—"coopetition," a fusion of cooperation and competition. Compelled or chosen, the limits of freedom are more than offset by the benefits of collaboration. The new ideal of the future is a reconstitution of identity, which will take the form of the collectivized individual who encloses self and other in the same person.

Mulgan further identifies three major laws of interconnectedness. The first is generally a corrective. The notion of technological advancement as discrediting what it ostensibly displaces is not borne out by patterns of evidence—throughout the twentieth century physical mobility and communications grew in tandem rather than as substitutes.

Electronic culture did not replace books; sales have increased. In fact, the availability of both appears online at Amazon.com. The growth of video conferencing ironically boosted the market for hotel conference centers. Economists claimed that 80 percent of economic growth in the 1950s was accounted for by technological change, but studies have shown the primary role played by ideas and knowledge growth in driving economic growth.

Thus, connexity tends to be cumulative. Each new medium of communication does not replace its predecessors so much as complement them. Thus, connexity rests on the recognition of recurrent coexistence. That is how so-called opposites or disconnects are perceived as being in tandem—as cooperating. Even in science, which tends to regularly throw out the past and to be noncumulative, what is really discarded are the conclusions, not the theories; the Greeks still haunt Darwin.

The second key law of increasing connectedness is the convergence of the world economy and world ecology. The environment has become the supreme advocate of interdependence and compelled a recognition of a single world, without borders, and perceived as a single whole from outer space. The same recognition is attributed to the global economy, which is a composite of world trade, world direct investments, global diffusion of technologies, and an integrated communications system. Indeed, the info-sphere has the same integrated qualities of the biosphere. In fact, Mulgan claims that we need new maps of the world to replace the standard ones of land masses as chosen by political masters. "The links matter as much as the territory, and our maps should show the volume of trade, of messages, or of movements of people. We need maps that can measure the ease of communication or travel in terms of how long it takes to send a message or to move a thing between two given points—giving us a map of the world made up of isomorphic lines, rapidly coming closer together over time, until most parts of the world are within twenty-four hours of each other in physical movement, and a few microseconds in terms of the movement of information" (23).

The intense economics of exchange in a global economy have created world prices for goods and services, where in the past there were only local prices. In fact, that is precisely the source of intimate competition: a plant in Ohio is aware of the price and the quality of the same product made in Korea, and, more seriously, so are its customers. Homo sapiens is increasingly becoming also Homo economicus, a person who defines himself as a series of multiple exchanges, who functions in an interconnected world made up of a lattice of contracts and reciprocal flows of goods and services.

The effort conceptually to master such complexity brought about the reinvention of political economy, which ironically existed as a single discipline in the nineteenth century and then was split wrongly into political science and economics. As a result, we have political scientists who know nothing about economics and economists who know little about politics. But unified again, the two disciplines have produced a significant body of research that affirms interconnectedness. Institutions of free trade have proven more effective than those designed to prevent or contain war and more diplomatic activity is now devoted to managing trade than to managing security. Global economy is thus as good, if not better, an advocate of peace as the United Nations, which is still a creation of barriers of sovereignty rather than their removal by interconnectedness. Another agent of global convergence is ecology. Pressure for ecological integration has become a critical force.

Finally, Mulgan's third law of convergence or connexity provides those like himself who are preoccupied with social, political, and economic design with a model to image and to design a self-organizing society, as opposed to one made up of separate self-organizing groups, the favorite isolated states of politicos. The philosophical idea that best expresses this ideal of a self-organizing society is self-creation. Rather than thinking of systems in relation to an external environment, we should see them as autonomous, circular, self-referential, and primarily concerned with their own organization and identity. The creation of a culture of autonomy suggests how a society might organize itself, adapting and evolving without the need for hierarchies and belief systems that stand above people, enforcing continuity and responsibility.

If each human life makes the transition from dependence through independence to interdependence, then societies can make the same transition, evolving into a common framework within which each element can take responsibility for itself and for the whole. To Mulgan, the promise of connexity is thus ultimately utopian.

Perhaps, the supreme spokesperson and articulator of the unification of all knowledge is Edward O. Wilson. In fact, his last book *Consilience* is subtitled "The Unity of Knowledge." In this role, he follows the lead of many who called the pursuit of the unity of all sciences the Ionian Enchantment. The roots go back at least to the sixth century BC and to Thales of Miletus, who, according to Aristotle, was the founder of the physical sciences. Wilson also acknowledges the pioneering work of Einstein, who, as "the architect of grand unification of physics, was Ionian to the core" (5).

But Wilson goes further in at least two respects. First, he takes as the scope of future convergence nothing less than all knowledge—not just the sciences but also the social sciences and the humanities: "Nothing fundamental separates the course of human history from the course of physical history" (9). Second, he envisions a coincidence of vision: namely, that the convergence of all knowledge will in effect be a creation story, tell us once and for all time who we are and why we are here, and thus test and affirm perhaps Holy Writ, the science of mythology. It will in essence constitute "the twenty-first century version of the struggle for the soul."

What is particularly instructive about Wilson's views is his identification of what has or may continue to prevent or compromise convergence. Thus, socially and politically we are typically unbalanced: "the vast majority of our political leaders are trained exclusively in the social sciences and humanities, and have little or no knowledge of the natural sciences" (13). And no one appears to be concerned about such a lopsided and fragmented situation. Nor is it often any better on the other side. There are physicists who really do not know what a gene is and biologists who are ignorant of string theory. The "fragmentation of expertise was further mirrored in the twentieth century by modernism in the arts and architecture" (39). In short, pieces are being passed off routinely as wholes across the board.

Wilson offers a real-life illustration of typical fragmentation. Governments generally are having a difficult time developing a policy to manage dwindling forest preserves of the world. Clearly, this is a multi-faceted problem. Minimally, it involves ecology, ethics, economics, and biology. Picture a quadrant in which each of these four fields inhabits one-quarter of the quadrant. The fact that four perspectives are identified in the first place is a major step forward, but it deteriorates rapidly from this point on. Immediately, arguments of jurisdiction or territoriality surface. That is rapidly followed by the ego of size and extent: how big or small each of the quadrants should be. In the process, mutual ignorance comes to the fore. Each field knows little or nothing about the others but enough to challenge pretensions to the throne and their being in the arena or quadrant in the first place.

Let's change the configuration a bit, suggests Wilson. Draw a series of concentric circles of different sizes that cut across all the intersections of the quadrant. That establishes the agenda of consilience. The smallest circle would be a set of minimum interfaces that would permit each discipline at least to acknowledge both its contributions and limitations. The larger more inclusive circles stress connections rather than separations. The largest circle offers the collective, cumulative, and convergent. The higher one goes in the food chain, the bigger the bite.

But there are few established ethical guidelines and those that exist generally are not shaped by ecological knowledge. The economics of sustainable yields is still a primitive art. What biologists know derives from short-term observations. The ecologists have been embarrassed by the boomerang of their premature death announcements as nature and animals often have bounded back. So there is a double problem: each discipline needs to deepen its own knowledge, and each discipline needs to know more about what they have in common. Consilience compels the highest, most encompassing and inclusive concentric circle that provides the optimum number of crossing and bridging points across boundaries.

It is Wilson's contention that, when a convergence agenda becomes paramount, then increasingly the likelihood is that concentric circles rather than quadrants will be the primary structure. But the agenda needs to be shaped by the leaders of each discipline in order to guide the research throughout the entire enterprise. The politics of positioning may be necessary for the interfacing benefits to be realized in daily exchange.

There are, for Wilson, four great chasms that need to be bridged. They are the conflict between the cultures of science and the humanities; the nature/nurture controversy; the physiology and psychology of the brain/mind; and the racial superiority/inferiority of world cultures. Not much progress has been made because each side believes it is right and the other is wrong. According to Wilson, they are both right. Indeed, the most difficult conflicts to solve are not between right and wrong, but a conflict of rights. Significantly, the way that Wilson seeks to bring about a more cooperative attitude and ultimately consensual convergence is in fact to reframe the opposition in terms that bring all the conflicts together under one roof. For example, the conflict between the two cultures is less the result of a fundamental antagonism than the creation of artificial territorial lines. If that were replaced by a "broader and mostly unexplored terrain inviting cooperative entry from both sides" (126), a larger, more formidable but more reconcilable version of the conflict would emerge. All human behavior and its artifacts are transmitted by culture. Biology has a share in the creation and transmission of culture: "The question remaining is how biology and culture interact, and in particular how they interact across all societies to create the commonalties of human nature. What, in final analysis, joins the deep, mostly genetic history of the species as a whole to the more recent cultural histories of its far-flung societies?" (126). Although Wilson admits that at the present time no one has the total solution, the answer already is apparent: "From diverse vantage points in biology, psychology and anthropology, they have conceived a process called gene–culture coevolution. In essense, the conception observes, first, that to genetic evolution the human lineage has added the parallel track of cultural evolution, and, second, that the two forms of evolution are linked" (127). Similarly, the great divides between different human societies have nothing to do with race, religion, or the innate superiority or inferiority of certain peoples. It has to do with the chasm that separates scientific from pre-scientific cultures.

Wilson accepts the notion that myth and religion function like science to explain who we are and why we are here. But without the knowledge of natural sciences, humans are trapped in a cognitive prison. Science, as opposed to art and religion (which seek to preserve mysteries), penetrates mystery in order to demonstrate the incredible order of a world shaped by natural selection. Wilson brings the same logic to the nature/nurture controversy: both clearly are involved and further genetic research, on the one hand, and research in psychology and sociology, on the other hand, will produce more precise allocations of nurture or nature situationally and perhaps even individually.

Finally, in this connection Wilson believes radically that Freud's explanations of dreams and unconscious behavior need to be suspended until sufficient empirical research has been conducted to verify or nullify his views. The causes and treatment of schizophrenia, which have eluded many psychologists, seem to be amenable more to a genetic explanation and appropriate psychological treatment.

Wilson is most tentative about the brain/mind duality. Wilson starts with the basic premise that "natural selection built the brain to survive in the world and only incidentally to understand it at a depth greater than is needed to survive" (61). Humans thus share with all other creatures the survival thrust of the brain. But to master both survival and achieve dominance at a higher level—in effect, to dominate the survival of all other creatures and the world of nature itself—the brain was compelled to create mind. But that does not mean that the mind or the intelligence gathering and analytical capacity of the mind was fundamentally different physically. Rather, it was different neurophysically. In other words, mind was still a scientific engine, not a soul or spirit. Indeed, current research needs "to tighten the connectedness between the events and laws of nature, and the physical basis of human thought processes" (65). The molecular biology of the learning process will considerably enhance the study and creation of artificial intelligence, as well as the embryonic field of artificial emotion.

Finally, Wilson believes that the three great areas of inquiry and convergence for the next twenty years will be mind, behavior, and ecology (95). Equally as important is the recognition that the ultimate goal of all science is "predictive synthesis," still in its infancy but extremely important and attainable. It is not achievable without enough empirically based demonstrations of consilience. But the substantial development of such evidence will be the emergence of predictive synthesis as the ultimate fruit of convergence.

What then are the yields of this examination of convergence as a mega-trend? There at least five. The most obvious is that convergence has the capacity to radically disturb not merely the branches but also the roots of all knowledge. Second, it is developmentally progressive and supports an epistemological and structural taxonomy not unlike Maslow's classic hierarchy. The following stages of evolution appear basic:

1. Similarity
2. Duality
3. Parallel
4. Paradox/Ambiguity
5. Cross-Overs
6. Integration
7. Synthesis
8. Convergence, Connexity, Consilience

Third, convergence provides the theoretical and empirical basis for understanding and anticipating a number of developments born of integration. These include the technology of theology; the creation of an internal pharmacy, brain chips, and the third intelligence; the appearance of the great convergence (the fusion of science and spirituality); and the pursuit of immortality.

Fourth, Mulgan took convergence into sociology, politics, and economics and envisioned interconnectedness as the antidote to excessive self-assertion by individuals and societies. His descriptions of the social benefits of connexity suggest that similar gains may be as possible and persuasive in the technological, scientific, and theological areas as well.

Finally, Edward O. Wilson offers resolutions to a number of the major debates of our time. In the process, he maintains that everything is linked, nothing is singular, and ultimately the physical, the

spiritual, and cultural expressions of human existence and definition shall be known in common. It is a faith based on strong empirical research and documentation, and it represents his vision of
the third century.

But if it is to happen with less rancor, the specialists need to become generalists and the generalists have to persuade the specialists
to join them. The first step of convergence thus always requires exchange. The intermediate stage involves interdependence. The last
step is always greater than the sum of all the cross-overs, including
what follows in the next chapter.

Oblique Leadership 24

S O MUCH EMPHASIS IS PUT UPON the ability of leaders to be decisive, to make the hard choices, to take problems head on, that perhaps we underestimate the need occasionally to side step, to be a little oblique—in short, to deflect. Postponement or procrastination is not what is being described here. Neither is the often illusory need for more data. Rather, a conscious effort is made by a leader to diagnose a situation and to select a different and alternative decision context or mode instead of the standard head-on, direct way of doing and deciding things.

What makes a decision oblique? What factors and possible consequences would a leader have to be willing to accept or endure?

1. It is not a rapid process. Indeed, it involves a bit of a journey. Specifically, the longest way around ultimately may be the shortest way home. It involves stepping back, sometimes relating or telling a story. It invites pause and patience.
2. It seeks to be inclusive. It unpredictably may involve opposites: being and becoming. It may be paradoxical. But it is not just a decision to do something. It always involves being something as well.
3. It is instructive. The decision is meant also to teach (including decision-making). The decision itself embodies the message. It invites reflection and deeper, less conventional thought.

4. It is affirmative. It leads to a renewal of commitment, of what is important and valued, of first principles. It is always aspirational and occasionally it is even spiritual.
5. It is a tribute to a leader as a student not only of the business but also of decision-making. Indeed, his awareness of multiple and alternative choices directly reflects not only his knowledge of the diversity of the organization and his role as the embodiment of its vision, but also his professional craft of leadership and capacity to model aspiration. It is his leadership signature.

What occasions invite oblique leadership? Although hopefully the five examples below will provide a number of the essential situational contexts, there are recurrent, almost archetypal situations that invite the exercise of reflective leadership.

One critical occasion involves the recognition that this particular situation cannot be limited to standard or routine matters but requires also selecting the high road. There is the need to return or recall first principles, the original vision and mission, why we are here and doing what we are doing in the first place—the core business. That, in turn, requires developing distance from the flux of the present and the crush of problem solving. In short, there is a need to carve out a space to make a different kind of decision.

Another occasion invariably has to do with the need for trust or rebuilding it. This is a particularly important restorative effort after downsizing, mergers, acquisitions, and so forth. A key related part of that reconstituting process is communications and the need to accurately and honestly read the divergence between official statements and the rumor mill.

Still another optimal situation is one in which the final decision will be a low-profile one. It will not be personalized as management or presidential; nor will it come on the scene brashly as policy. It will simply be a new way of doing things. It will be neutral, nonjudgmental, and minimal. It will be a mechanism, produced often by executive decision but oblique enough to float free on its own without prejudice or intimidation.

Below are examples of leadership by indirection. Obviously, more could be added, but the list seeks to be representative of this kind of decision-making, as well as the different environments in which they can and do occur. In most cases, a typicality of focus is sought so that, although the particular organization and industry may not be that of the reader, the issue and approach are hopefully generic.

Example 1

A key current illustration involves addressing the increasingly urgent problem of stirring creativity and innovation. One company used the direct approach, which involved the decision of the vice president of marketing to assemble an innovation committee comprised of one elected representative from each division of the company.

The vice president of marketing gave the committee its charge, which included guidelines, timetables, and financial incentives for results. A facilitator/consultant was also assigned to the committee who had promised the vice president that he would write up for publication this successful effort of his. Six months later the conclusion was that the effort failed. Some good ideas for improvement were developed, but these fell so far short of achieving the goals that they were unheeded. The official explanation was that the failure was largely due to the apathy of the employees, who did not take the opportunity seriously and who regarded the financial incentives as insufficient to motivate.

A different, more oblique approach and decision of another company recognized that the issue of creativity or innovation is not a routine matter and requires some distance, some more prefatory considerations. The first dimension of distant assumption was that the solution is not always to be found close to the problem. That was followed by the tough question that no one could or wanted to answer: "Is everyone creative?" Although skirted at this point, that question generated a standard for the solution: it had somehow to sort out the answer to that question over time. Above all, what signaled an initial indirect, deflective, and reflective approach was the question "What motivates creativity?"

That question stopped everything. All had to step back and look at a bigger whole. The perspective was more challenging especially because what emerged was the answer that nothing motivates creativity. Creativity is not subject to external prodding, timetables, or financial lures. Creativity is curiosity. And curiosity is self-generating. If a company is persuaded that it has creative people and/or that it cannot survive without innovation, then it needs to follow the wonderfully oblique decision made by 3M Company. It was announced that every employee was free to work on any new or creative project that interested them, but they could not spend more than 15 percent of their total time on the project and certainly not at the expense of completing their regular work assignments. It worked like a charm. The results were astounding. And productivity improved because all assignments still were completed on time.

Why was this indirect solution so much better than the direct one? The most obvious immediate value was the generous assumption that everyone in the organization was creative and the determination of what form that would take would be self-selecting. There were no announced projects that were sanctioned. That subject came up only as a follow-up concern: "Can I work on anything I want?" The answer promptly was "Yes." So a broad approach with no strings attached led to a comprehensive embrace of the opportunity. Then, with feigned management arbitrariness and parental control, a limit of 15 percent was imposed, the characteristic knee-jerk sign of an uncreative administration.

The oblique decision succeeded for two reasons. First, the decision was not directive but permissive. That way no one had to engage in the counterproductive task of determining who was creative and who was not. The assumption is that everyone was. And to test that only required the decision-maker to step back and create the space for creativity to fill and hopefully flourish. But it was not permitted to become license. That was the only concession offered to directive control. Second, there were no financial incentives offered for creativity because money is never what creativity is all about in the first place. Moreover, instead of worrying what motivates creativity, the oblique approach shifted to what stirs it. And even then it was not prescriptive.

In effect, then, all oblique decisions are environmental. Rather than direct or manipulate employees, the focus is on creating a permissive but circumscribed space for people to fill in a manner that allows for and encourages total differentiation and individuality. In fact, creating a stable and secure environment in general is the most supportive way of stimulating creativity and productivity.

Secure environments make companies attractive to work for. Many have a non-layoff policy; the rest have found other ways of promoting job stability. Job jeopardy also has resulted in increased health benefits costs of ailing and even dysfunctional employees. In short, leaders need to curb their need to appear as saviors or infallible know-it-alls. Instead they need to recognize that, although shaping the environment may be less glamorous or charismatic, it encourages choice, comfort, and creativity.

Example 2

Perhaps surprisingly, an excellent example of oblique leadership set in a context of war occurs in the recent film *Saving Private Ryan*. Although there are at least three instances where decision-making is tangential, the first one sets the tone for the others—indeed, for the entire film. It is discovered that three of four Ryan brothers have been killed in action. During the last week the remaining brother had parachuted behind enemy lines and his whereabouts are unknown. The case comes before General George Marshall for a final decision. His aides present strong arguments against finding and sending the surviving Ryan brother back home. His military aide de camp points out that no one knows where he is and that those who search for him may become causalities themselves. The PR officer points out that other families have suffered, perhaps not as much as the Ryans, but they too would expect their survivors to be brought back home.

Marshall listens to all these persuasive arguments but says nothing. He slowly goes behind his desk and pulls out a Bible. But unexpectedly he pulls out a piece of paper from which he starts to read. It is a letter to a Mrs. Bixby, who lost four sons in combat. The writer lamely and apologetically seeks to console her and to offer her the condolences and deep thanks of a grateful country. The letter is from Abraham Lincoln. General Marshall does not say another word. The aides bow their heads in agreement. The decision to rescue Private Ryan has been made by Abraham Lincoln. Couldn't Marshall have basically said the same thing and made the same decision? Of course, but why is the oblique leadership choice so much more effective?

The obvious factor is that there is no ego involved, no grandstanding patriotism, no attention-grabbing or deflecting posturing. That keeps the focus where it has to be: on Mrs. Ryan. In addition, because it is not within her power to make that decision, someone else or some other power has to act as her advocate. In other words, oblique leadership recognizes that the decision that has to be made has to be taken out of the hands of the decision-maker and given to a more removed, higher authority—in this case, Lincoln and the United States.

But perhaps the key source of power of tangential decision-making is the return to first principles—to why we are fighting this war in the first place, to what business are we really in, to what is a vision and our mission. Moreover, it is only the leader or the CEO who can invoke the fundamental rationale for an organization's existence—not what we do, but why we do it. His task always is to read certain decision situations carefully and be ready to call upon Abraham Lincoln to carry the day.

Example 3

Performance appraisal probably has never and may never enjoy good press. Certainly, it has erred more than it has been right. But a number of years ago it spawned an equally questionable companion process called management by objectives (MBO). The rationale was obvious. There was a crying need to produce comprehensive job descriptions for everyone; otherwise the appraisal process could not be benchmarked. Then, too, to make it more directive the process had to identify the management objectives of each employee, so that he would have a clear notion of what he was responsible for and could be managed.

Did it work? Yes and no. On the one hand, it brought greater sanity, conformity, and clarity to the review process. Employees knew what their goals were and managers were thus better able to manage and evaluate people according to their goals. The other important benefit was that when a new task or initiative surfaced, it was a relatively easy matter to identify the talent that was needed to attack the problem. But, ironically, in its very success MBO betrayed a fundamental flaw.

A number of managers began to be disturbed by a counterproductive pattern of exclusion that surfaced. Managers who took pride in knowing the talents of their people found to their surprise that some people who they thought would be perfect for certain task forces were excluded on the basis of their MBO profile. In addition, in a number of cases, those selected to work on the new initiative reinforced the manager's perception by asking why so-and-so was not included. The answer that their MBO did not make them eligible for the task led to an initial disenchantment with the profile. Some managers even pushed testing MBO further by asking employees to identify who they believed should be on a special problem-solving team. What emerged was that at least half of those nominated to serve would not have been actively considered according to their MBO. Gradually MBO thus became discredited and unfortunately the response was to throw the baby out with the bathwater.

The wall of MBO excluded as much as it included. A high price of talent potentially wasted or untapped was paid for clarity. Performance appraisal was certainly neater and more manageable, but it fell far short of employee improvement and development, which is really what the entire process is all about in the first place.

The value of this example is that it dramatizes the need in all situations of employee growth to balance the direct and the indirect, the prescribed and the collaborative. If a wall is to be put in place it should have gates that swing both ways. Or better still, it should be a parlay point where both sides, manager and worker, routinely negotiate growth and productivity. If one conceives of leadership as solely a decisive act, one is always acting and deciding. But if one conceives of it as a mixture of the direct and the oblique, then the decision-maker controls but he also may decide to share control.

Job descriptions are helpful but not if they imprison and make less of what an employee is and can contribute. Subtle writers like Frost value the contributions of readers, so they create room and roles to invite those responses. Leaders are storytellers. They need audiences. The difference is whether you want obedience or creativity. Oblique decisions always are empowering.

Kendall Murphy, author and management consultant, tells a marvelous story about himself that illustrates another key dimension of tangential decision-making. A number of years ago, while he was working for Pacific Bell, he was promoted to run a division of some six hundred employees. It was a problem division. Productivity was low; so was morale. Murphy was no stranger to difficulties of this sort. He had turned around two other smaller units. Clearly, that is why he was chosen to head up this new larger unit. But because of its size and the need to review such a sizable number of employees, and because it involved some highly technical operations that Murphy hoped to understand and eventually master, he decided to go slow. He did not take over meetings but allowed his subheads to run their own meetings as they had in the past. He attended every one, of course, and often asked questions.

The month went by quickly, and to his surprise he began to notice significant improvements in the division. Equally as important, so did some of his fellow managers and superiors. He was puzzled. He called his subheads together for a meeting. They were in high spirits. Kendall did not want to give away that he was surprised at what had happened. So instead of asking how it happened, he sought their input on how to keep up the momentum. The response was this: "Just keep asking those good questions."

Without being fully aware of it, Kendall was asking some basic questions that had never been asked before. Moreover, they were open-ended questions that did not imply that he had the answers. The subheads took the questions seriously and developed with their own subordinates action responses to the questions.

The net result was the decision to change their ways. What this example dramatizes is the indirect role of the leader as an asker of questions as opposed to the direct role of a giver of answers. Without fully knowing it, Murphy had raised his questions to the level of the state of the art because the questions probed, elicited, and generated actions as the answers.

Example 4

The last illustration is admittedly a stretch, almost a cosmic reach. It has to do with the gradual appearance of metaphors for business organizations that are not the conventional military, new frontier, or paternal paradigms of the past. They are less inspired by Newton as by Rachel Carson; they are less mechanical arrangement of parts and more fluid, even convoluted and more self-enfolding. Specific versions include Wheatley's metaphor of the river as fluid structural model; of Hardin Craig's tragedy of the commons as the collective metaphor of what is held in common; and the model of the rain forest as a human ecosystem as described by Taichi Kiuchi.

In all these cases, the difference is signaled by a shift from what humans do to alter and improve nature and thus create what did not exist before, to the processes and operations we inherited collectively from the planet Earth. In both instances, the key role is that of the designer. In the first instance what is celebrated is the ingenuity and creativity of human design. This is inventive, intrusive, and interventionist in nature. It is what has been called in this discussion the direct decision-making approach.

But the new metaphors celebrate the secrets of wholes—of the origins of rivers and their terminus into the oceans; of lands held in common that fail because of lack of community and communication; and of rain forests whose capital is precisely in their complex and delicate design. In other words, not unlike all the examples we have explored, the decision is shared with another leader or leading force so that negotiation and collaboration can come to a mutual decision. The oblique leader recognizes that nature has to be brought back to the negotiating table and be given equal time with Newton and others. Nature here is the equivalent of Abraham Lincoln.

The case for oblique leadership and tangential decision-making should not devalue or minimize the case for direct, decisive, directional leadership and decision-making. Instead, what is suggested is that strong leaders can be even stronger if they share power and vision with the CEO of 3M, Abraham Lincoln, Kendall Murphy, Robert Frost, and Rachel Carson. Perhaps this way it will be less lonely at the top and happier at the middle and the bottom as well. The lateral mind and leader are special.

The Integrative Leader's Lateral Mind 25

Roles
Uniter
Intersecter
Converger
Asking Why
Includer
Synergist
Knowledge Pusher
Frontier Challenger

THE INTEGRATIVE LEADER IS fascinated by what is not there or is disturbingly missing or by what is there but does not fit or add up or make sense. His instinct regularly is to assume that there is more than meets the eye, that underneath and alongside the dynamics of all operations and group behaviors lurks a secret sharer—an invisible partner that holds everything together, in balance, and grants coherence. Where do such suspicions come from? From a long history of trying to explain and manage reality—of trying to comprehend what men and their machines and systems have designed to persuade us that all is known and works and no pieces are left out.

But it is precisely the ineptitude or the uncaring nature of the solution, its lopsided favoring of one group over others, and, above all, the fact that we are forced to work with an imperfect and inadequate model that leads the integrative leader to press the stop button and bring all to a halt.

He is thus often resented. Why can't he leave well enough alone? Why is he always a "yes, but" type? It is not as if he already has the answer. All he has is his intuitive misgiving that it does not compute. Besides, he insists that, when something is as basic as how a company should organize and structure itself and how it should ask others to join it in a mutual enterprise, it should make sense and be equitable—even somehow resemble the laws of nature or the universe—and should not be so blatantly imperfect as to compel choosing between Tweedledee and Tweedledum as the lesser of two evils. Indeed, it is the citation of such successful past examples of rejecting false alternatives that often carries the day and permits unbridled inquiry.

It thus would not be an exaggeration to label all such seekers as perfectionists. In fact, they have a great deal in common with all the traditional seekers of the holy grail, the elixir of life, the unified field theory, the leadership gene—with any and all those seeking the fountain of youth. Indeed, it is precisely such visions that explain their power to attract loyal followers and to create institutional homes and centers. In the case of Edison, he was a presiding genius with charisma, but in a number of other instances it is an ideology such as global sustainability or the Copenhagen think tank of future studies. Indeed, to appreciate the extent to which the integrative spirit is alive and well, consider all the focused centers all over the world engaged in independent inquiry, and representing a research focus not only equal to that of the universities but also more unfettered and daring. In this institutional sense, the world is not only being led by integrative leaders of great merit, but its followers have also been trained in the reality of secret intersectors.

Focus
More
Bigger
More Inclusive
Holistics
360

Virtual Teaming
Singularity

In many ways the operating theory of integrative knowledge is that everything is connected to everything else—exactly how is not known but the clear direction is finding the connectors. That is why the framework of the integrative is always the more, the bigger, the more inclusive, the 360, the holistic. It may occur at enormous or tiny ends of the spectrum—huge atomic colliders, Hubble telescopes, or nano-technology—but the key is that they are all miniatures of the whole. They render absolute complexity available and solvable.

What then sets the integrative leader apart? If one were to set up a leadership development program, what would be involved? Already noted is the common component of vision, but integrative vision is less self-serving; it has a more generous, overflowing, humanitarian dimension to it. That is so because it was triggered by the harmful shortcuts and preferential priorities of an unfairly designed, short-sighted system that required bold and comprehensive correctives.

Modes

Lateral Thinking
Cross-Thinking
Intersectional Knowledge
Human-Machine Identity
Direction
Left and Right
Up and Down
Diagonal and Across
Circular

In addition, the emerging integrative leader has to be introduced to lateral thinking—how to slide across the page from left to right, how to read like ancient Hebrews from right to left, how to read like the Japanese up and down in columns, how to build up words like the Germans, how to live within and think in spreadsheets, how to understand Aristotle's injunction to begin *in media res*, and what are the only two optimum points for rendering an action, for meditation of soft breathing, and so forth.

Next he has to be exposed to cross-knowledge: biology and chemistry and then biochemistry, economics and politics and then political economy, markets and votes—all the crosscurrents that are not taught. Culturally driven beliefs. Science of demographics. Human-machine relationships.

Outcomes

New Organizational Composites
New Human Amalgams
New Hybrids

What are the typical creations of integrative institutions and leaders? They are not so much new as discovered designs—the secret, unified wholes. For all their dreamy ways and allegiances, they always value and produce works designed to live and function intelligently, not in some "never never land," but in this world with real people—tangible and workable relationships for conducting human affairs. All integrative types are compulsive questioners. They continue in more focused form the constant and often annoying whys of childhood. Kendall Murphy's story of his experience at Pacific Bell included in chapter 24, and the outcomes that resulted from his questioning, illustrates the integrative leader in action.

Developing an Innovation Quotient   **26**

THE INNOVATOR

INNOVATION REQUIRES A SPECIAL strategy of deflection. It should not be attacked head-on but, instead, surrounded with multiple and reinforcing approaches—three in particular: ideas, questions, and multiple intelligence. Innovation is too elusive and too clever to be obviously tricked into making itself easily available or usable. Innovation is an artful dodger that eludes the grasp of singular or linear sequential approaches. But it can be accessed by ideas, questions, and multiple intelligence.

Even Thomas Edison found creativity intimidating. So, rather than storm the barricades, he settled for thresholds to innovation. He turned instead to ideas. But lest matters remain too unspecified or be allowed to drift without closure, he divided ideas into two types: major and minor. He required that he and all his fellow inventors operate on a quota and timetable system. Edison's was modest: one major and six minor ideas within six months. One would have expected Edison to be more ambitious until one discerns how exacting his definition of ideas was. They were to be genuinely new, unborrowed, and haunting. They could not be rehashed or absorbed from anyone else. And they could not offer any easy resolution or peace.

Edison kept an idea diary, as did many of his coworkers. The pages following the recording of the original idea were filled with many revisions, twists, and turns, as if the idea is writhing in agony to finally express and release itself in unexpected clarity. At that point, the idea crossed the threshold into the laboratory. That is where innovation was born.

But, of course, not always. Some ideas remained stuck in an undeveloped or unapplied state. Others cluster, complicate, and confuse each other, producing a rich impasse. Like orphans or old lovers, they were even abandoned and remained unfinished still lifes. To be sure, some submerged into the unconscious, there to be suspended permanently or until another idea summoned their reengagement and resurfacing. But so many shared a fate of suspension that one can better understand why Edison settled for only one major idea and six minor ones. Only the strongest and most tenacious could survive the idea gauntlet. And even some of those subsequently failed to see the light of day.

Using Edison as our model and ideas as the means to innovation, what then are the essential ingredients of an intellectual IQ—an ideas quotient? Minimally, three: curiosity, persistence, and surprise.

The dilemma is that idea-curiosity is rare in adults, especially relating to big ideas. Like enthusiasm and delight, it has been usually disciplined out of us during our early years in school. The MBA continues the process by enshrining the conventional current holies. To rediscover the power and spontaneity of idea-curiosity requires an understanding of the thinking and learning processes of childhood.

A child expresses his curiosity through play. Learning is child's play. But although that was acceptable before school (sometimes, sadly, not even then), formal schooling marks the time to put away our play and get down to real work. School, like a job, is serious business and cannot be taken lightly. It perhaps recalls Huck Finn's difficult question of Tom Sawyer: "Why is it that kids are good but many adults are bad?" Tom answers philosophically: "They just grow up." Shortly after that, Huck decides not to be civilized by Aunt Sally but instead lights out for the territory ahead—the West—so that he can remain permanently a child.

The key to recovering curiosity is to reintroduce serious and exacting play into work—to bring to the job what we do outside of the job. The current preoccupation with balancing work and life might be enriched and better directed by such an exchange. Frost rightly claimed, "My ambition is to make my avocation my vocation and my vocation my avocation." To make play work means process-driven training: scenarios, simulations, role-playing, scripting, teaming—all hands-on. But it all has to be involving, exhibit verisimilitude, and be work-specific. Generic trust exercises won't cut it. The goal is to refresh the eyes, ears, and even the heart to perceive the daily, ordinary, and habitual exchanges of work with a child's way of problem stating and solving.

Play has to be serious, not a trivial pursuit or indulgence. It uses a child's mind to roam and do mischief in the adult world of knowledge, ideas, and work assumptions. But because it is always directed toward problem solving, play needs to generate adult ideas and engage adult persistence lest the child's capacity for distraction and novelty rule. An idea thus becomes child's play grown up. It is big but focused, generalized but detailed, fuses the forest and the trees. Adult persistence appears in application. That extends and disciplines play into work. Curiosity is preserved but now is applied to problem solving. Adult takeover is signaled by the appearance of ideas, but all movement forward is cumulative. Play is not left behind but subsumed. The child and adult coexist. The recovery is so seamless that it is not possible to determine where the one begins and the other leaves off. Innovation, in short, is born of the fusion of ideas and play or rather idea-play.

Another characteristic of the curiosity of the child is asking questions, endlessly, although often that capacity is sadly compromised. Impatient schooling, busy parents at home, and supervisors at work sadly squelch and suppress questions. Indeed, when frowns or other forms of disapproval appear, the questions often stop being asked altogether. Then, too, mixed signals often reinforce silence: a question is asked by one of the bright rising stars and is immediately welcomed, when earlier exactly the same one put forth by one less favored was ignored. Gradually, fear and fairness produce silence. The famous "the road not taken" becomes "the question not asked."

Questioning is another form of play. In the child it carries no limits or responsibility. Questions just pour out, pell-mell, in hit-and-miss fashion. They beget others ad infinitum that roam all over the place. But that is what play is. It has no purpose other than being playful. But questions are curiosity embodied in language. As such, it is the way the child thinks and the way he finds and expresses his first ideas and forms his first relationships.

Questions and ideas need not only to be paired but also to become avenues to and versions of each other. The idea quotient (IQ) has to be supplemented with a question quotient (QQ). The focus on innovation has to involve stirring systematic questioning technique and applications. The larger institutional goal is to create a questioning culture.

Questioning has a number of creative functions and applications. First, it assumes there are answers to questions. When Ben-Gurion was asked shortly after Israel became a nation what it was like to be prime minister, he answered with a question: "What is it like to be prime minister of a country in which everyone thinks he is the prime minister?" Other than being politically astute, the point of using a question to respond to a question is to shift the focus from the leader to those ostensibly being led and thus provide more information than we would have had if the question was simply and directly answered. In other words, answering questions with questions builds and expands the knowledge base. It is a data-gathering process. It also can be an innovating process when the question is given over to the problem.

Questions also facilitate changing identities. They can structure cross-over. They enable the problem solver to ask how the problem would solve itself and then go quiet and listen to the answer. Innovation often requires being a conduit, a messenger taking orders. The invention is always bigger than the inventor. But even when questions do not yield solutions, they often gather the information that is the key to problem solving. Perhaps, the classic expression of that yield was the typical way Louis B. Mayer began his conversations: "For your information, let me ask you a question."

Questions are tyrannical. They demand answers. And if the questions are tough and have been worked up to the state of the art, they can generate information that expands significantly the knowledge base. For example, one exercise in innovation training that conveys both the informational and creative power of questioning would require all attendees to assemble a list of frequently asked questions for a new product or process. Or to anticipate and prepare a Q&A

list for a stockholders meeting, a merger, or the press. Varying the audience ups the extent, range, and depth of the questions but all expose ignorance, limited understanding, and questionable assumptions. And all of these singly or collectively preclude innovation.

If the holy grail is granted only to the pure of heart, innovation comes only to the endless questioners. Ignorance and ego mutually block or blunt the process. Questions take care of both by taking us outside of the box of ourselves and of limiting assumptions. The process is one of increasingly using information and insight to bring about a coincidence of inventor and invention, of problem and solution.

Questions also can be systematically structured. The Japanese approach to problem solving involves getting at the root cause. When something breaks down or targets are not met, the Japanese ask "Why?" at least five times to reach bedrock. The limits of each partial answer and stage compel further inquiry until finality occurs. Because such questioning is regarded as a neutral agent of inquiry by all, the blame, shame, and gotcha-game are not involved. Indeed, if such questioning becomes a norm, it also could become company culture—its mission.

The classic formula of problem solving is know-what, know-how and know-why. The last needs to be first. Questions and ideas need to drive everything else. And, further, when that is done collectively and systematically, it leads to information sharing, which ultimately evolves into leadership sharing. If an organization is stuck and asks, "When was the last time we came up with a new idea?" then it is time to develop a questioning culture—if for no other reason, then not to be paralyzed by such an unanswered question.

Questions can start new businesses and tap new markets, as well as maintain, renew, and energize existing ones. And if they don't, companies may wake up one morning to find their breakfast eaten by another whose new ideas generated quality questions as their competitive edge.

One last member of the innovative trinity of ideas and questions needs to be brought into play. And that involves multiple intelligences (MI), especially as identified and defined by its original inventor, Howard Gardner. Aside from explicitly linking MI to creativity, Gardner enriches the entire process of innovation by bringing minimally two dimensions to bear on training. The first requires the recognition that every employee is multiply talented. The second shifts the question from "How smart am I?" to "How am I smart?" That change of focus from standard and singular IQ to a process-oriented and multiple world of ideas and questions signals a change from analysis to creativity, from incremental productivity to discontinuous innovation. What Gardner argued is that we are not only adaptive but also multiply so. We grow and know in many and diverse ways and along multiple learning pathways. Finally, the internal cognitive world, which stirs creativity, is as busy and interactive as what it creates. Gardner conceded that Western civilization in general had achieved distinction for the most part through linguistically driven analysis. But he argued that not only was more involved, but that what often was passed off as solely the process of verbal dominance was in reality multiply produced. Indeed, the driving spark was often nonverbal.

In his seminal work *Frames of Mind* (1983), Gardner identified seven, and later eight, basic intelligences: linguistic, musical, logical-mathematical, spatial, bodily-kinesthetic, interpersonal, intrapersonal, and naturalist. In later discussions of optimal human adaptability, Gardner stresses the existential and the futuristic, rounding it out to ten.

What does MI bring to innovation?

- All humans are multiply configured.
- The design is wired in the brain and biology.
- Current IQ is singular and thus reductive. It measures only linguistic intelligence.
- All intelligences are multiply operative in preschool children.
- They appear as playful development of simple and basic ideas and questions.
- Such a gradually expanding knowledge base is common to all children and constitutes the life-long legacy of the species.
- The three principal and preferred activities of MI are communication (socialization), problem solving, and creativity.
- But they all are routinely goal-directed and directional.
- When schools build on to the acquired common knowledge base, continue to tap the multiple talents that produced it, and

set end goals of inquiry and achievement focused on optimal adaptability, this brings fully into play the three fundamental activities of communication, problem solving, and creativity.
• Problem solving and creativity are two sides of the same coin.

How then can MI be used to stir and advance innovation? One of its principal contributions is serving as a constant multiplier. The intelligences constitute a circular checklist of problem definition. Each intelligence would generate its own version. The problem would thus be surrounded and immediately enriched by a cast of characters and a range of statements that ideally would be 360 degrees. Later on such a comprehensive matrix can be flipped over and applied to the solution.

Routinely, such a dynamic also establishes or renews each employee's relationships with different and many ways of knowing, thinking, and learning. Access to a richer interior world is initially bracing, subsequently familiar, and regularly extending. Each employee is bigger and thus more equal and fortified to stretch work tasks and goals.

The inherent interoperability of MI also facilitates cross-overs of perspective and function. It can do so because it can not only externally display the multiple complexities of the company in miniature, but also make them interoperable. MI would have considerably eased the exchange of positions of the automotive engineers and the battery. And because Gardner has factored in the interpersonal and intrapersonal, the groundwork for incorporating emotional intelligence also has been laid and even anticipated.

Above all, MI ups the ante. It requires the three basic activities to be constantly reciprocal, almost interchangeable. Communications has to be problem solving and creative. Problem solving has to be communicative and innovative. Creativity must exhibit communicality and solve problems. Ordinarily, each task would be a separate operation, but in MI's enriched environment they are all contiguous and interfacing.

The MI world is always finally holistic, and its innovative creations, when and if they come, emerge fully formed and complete. Singular approaches limited to singular intelligence routinely pass off halves as wholes. If innovation is the company mission, MI constitutes its vision.

In summary then three changes are being advocated. First, if innovation can be taught, it can be done so only obliquely and through kinship allies. The thresholds proposed are those of ideas, questions, and multiple intelligences. All three lend themselves to systemic application and thus not only offer uniform and comprehensive use across the board but also are amenable and receptive to individual and company original signatures.

Second, for innovation to take hold and be a driving force, it must bring together or unite three essentials: communication, problem solving, and creativity. Reciprocity between all three will produce a holistic vision, which ultimately may be the most enduring, embracing, and reverberating innovation of all to all.

Third, choose an innovation leader. When the universe is disturbed, everything changes including the definition of best practices. Indeed, the first task of the leader is to note that these are temporary versions of perfection and perhaps good starting points but certainly not end points.

But his hardest task is to remove the barriers to involvement and persuade his administrative colleagues to let the people go—to turn innovation over to the workforce. That would give a new meaning and application to the notion of distributed leadership and honor the special culture-creating vision of the innovation leader. That leader asks questions on behalf of his organization perhaps along the following lines:

1. To what extent do organizations contribute and inhibit innovation?
2. What is the general relationship between innovation and general intelligence? Between IQ and MI? How smart am I to how am I smart?
3. If innovation cannot be measured or taught or if the state of the art is beyond us permanently or temporarily, what can be offered reassuringly in the meantime? What proximate thresholds can be tapped?

4. Develop an organizational innovation agenda:

1. Preservation and the Present
A. Internal
Status Quo Operational Questions: What does it take for us to preserve present market share?
B. External
Market Question: What is our competitive edge? What about the competitive edge of our competitors?
2. Anticipatory and Short Terms
If our competitors already have eaten our breakfast or lunch, how do we protect our dinner?
3. Innovation Question, Timeless or Omnipresent Wild Card, Out of Left Field
What and who has the potential to put us out of business?

5. Future questions:

How do companies get blind-sided? What are our blind spots?
Is the threat inside not outside the gates?
What is our look-ahead IQ?
Is our leader out there?

Innovation Range: Three Professionals and Their Process Preferences   **27**

THE NEED FOR INNOVATION IS obvious; how to do it is not. To begin with, the subject is still beset by the perennial question of whether it should be across the board or limited to select types. Then too there is the question of the role of company culture and the extent to which its support of innovation is sufficient to determine happy outcomes. What direction should training take? Generic or customized? Can innovation potential even be measured, let alone isolated, in initial interviews? Lastly, what shapes creative company cultures? Above all, with innovation, should not answers always emanate from a focus not on external products but rather internal process—on who embraces its pursuit, how it evolves, and what are the contributions of company culture to its emergence?

The task is not an easy one largely because it involves acknowledging an underlying dynamic that generally exceeds leadership concepts. Thus, typically, professionals are defined primarily by what they possess not by what they favor—in this case, by the problems and processes they characteristically or compulsively choose. But preference also often generates repetition and reputation. A number of professionals are singled out as the in-house go-to expert or guru for certain kinds of problems, others by their special past experiences, assignments, or networks, and a few by their knowledge of research sources. But whatever their original education, training, or specialty, the one that is developed and mastered trumps all. It becomes their signature—their individual best practice. And the preferences chosen in effect define their mission, sometimes their passion.

Of course, such branding does not just happen. It evolves gradually, over time, often accompanied by false starts or inadequate outcomes. In short, specialization and its performance distinction are ruled imperfectly by success, as well as trial and error. But what finally imparts special shape and direction is the purposeful inter-relationship that exists between professionals, problems, and processes. Moreover, that dynamic when describable may generate not only answers to the above questions but also a model of innovation behaviors to follow. But a number of obstacles stand in the way, not the least of which is the expectation of uniformity—of "one size fits all."

Not all professionals are innovative. Not all problems require creativity. And not all processes facilitate innovation. Indeed, professionals are defined by the problems and the means they choose to employ. To be sure, that choice often is dictated or influenced by the discipline of each professional, and by the culture of their education, training, and work experience. But such determiners do not alter diversity. Difficult though it may be for some to admit, not all Ivy League MBAs are innovative. In short, the key across-the-board discrimination required is to designate which configuration of professional, problem, and process relationships optimizes innovation and which ones do not.

Such discriminations require profiling—in this case, problem profiling or problem triage. The extremes are quickly defined: run-of-the-mill problems and exceptions to the rule. Those in between are held aside to be subsequently sorted out and assigned to one of the original two. The deciding factor is whether the problem is processable by standard in-house procedures. If so, then although it may be designated as a somewhat more complex variation on a theme, it is still finally dispatched to the standard musical category. Or, if it is not, then it may be left in limbo for awhile, later revisited or finally, although reluctantly, designated an enigma.

But the triage process, though critical, is not infallible or unbiased. Mistakes are made and underestimates regularly occur. Indeed, over time they acquire and reflect a pattern. Namely, many companies and professionals are risk averse. Although that may take many forms, in this context it leads to designating problems as ordinary when they are uniquely daunting. Typically, problems are not given their just due because of inadequacy: it exceeds our calipers—or hierarchy; it is regarded as too small, inconsequential, or irrelevant to the mainstream of what typically is confronted. Strangely, such devaluation or trivializing is often covered up by bravado—by proudly proclaiming that we are a match for whatever is thrown at us or with the reassuring estimate that nearly all of that which has been successfully solved before leaves little left to trouble us.

But the truth is otherwise: Problems typically sort themselves out following the 80-20 rule. Most are garden variety, familiar, and re-current. They are feel-good challenges that routinely fold over and give up their solution without a fight. Not so the more exotic in-your-face disturbers of the peace that won't go away or be easily pacified. They stick in your craw and lead to sleepless nights. These one-of-a-kind challenges are not just new; they are differently new. They even may bear the face and force of paradigm shift, and such adjustment of perception may alter the percentage allocation and the degree of difficulty. In addition, because of current pressures of com-petition and loss of market share, some companies driven to the wall may claim that the innovation ante is now upped to 30 or even 50 percent of the whole—that such a business tsunami results in a call to rally not just for a select few but for all the troops to respond to the call for life-saving innovation.

But less panic and more precision is needed to save the day. Specifically, the key corrective and diagnostic required still remains the dynamic relationship between professionals, problems, and pro-cesses and how problem definition and solution options are driven by professional preferences and the favored choices of company cultures. At the heart of that relationship and what finally defines its yield is professional choice. Not inappropriately, triage may also serve to identify the following three basic types of professionals and their respective ideologies.

The Applier: The Continuity of Recurrency

Let us call him Mike. Companies could find no more exemplary embodiment of competency than this kind of problem solver and manager of problem-solving teams. Vigorous and rigorous, Mike is a supreme advocate of the capacity of a dedicated and disciplined workforce to be equal to any and all tasks. But he is also aware of the need constantly to update and upgrade, and thus not only regularly endorses training but also suggests its content.

To be sure, he finds it difficult to manage when layoffs occur and when such thinning out brings about basic gaps in skill sets. A hiring freeze and the limits of training to offset such deficiencies jeopardize the importance of competency and continuity. But most troubling is the loss or erosion of the culture of company loyalty. Its persistence and pervasiveness may make the prospect of retirement attractive.

Mike, like Ecclesiastes, operates under the assumption that there is nothing new under the sun and that the way we have customarily processed change and challenge is sufficient. In fact, he would claim that success occurs in more than 90 percent of the cases. And when or if it fails to work, the fault lies not in the process but in its application. His repeated call is to go back to square one and to apply due diligence. He is vigilant about detecting shortcuts or relying on dirty data. Indeed, when it still may not work even with all the correctives factored in, then he concludes that we don't know enough—that we need more data— even though we may reach the point where we never have enough.

Sadly, this stalwart of standards is the enemy of innovation. He regularly affirms the status quo of problem identification, processing, and solving and asserts at every meeting that all we need to do is to return to basics and core competencies. As a professional, his preferences are for problems that are familiar and of a piece—and that are aligned and in synch with the tried and tested processes that have been the source of success. Indeed, success turns out to be his supreme obstacle. A long record and history of spectacular achievement is trotted out to clinch his case. But seldom or never are such best practices found by Mike to be ironically imprisoning and paralyzing. When the Mikes are among the retiring baby boomers, although we typically may lament their departure and the loss of institutional memory or know-how, from the point of view of innovation it may be a necessary cleaning of the house essential to embracing a creative kind of problem solving. The generation liberated from Egypt was not the one to enter the promised land.

The Adapter—The Cutting Edge of Constant Currency

Let us call this one Sheila. Like Mike, Sheila values constancy, except in her case it is that of constant change. If Mike leans too heavily on the past, Sheila is embedded completely in the present. In fact, she regards the new as the now of the future. No one can match her busy and often dizzying gathering and cataloging of cutting-edge best practices. Totally on top of her game, she is a tireless researcher of industry patterns and those of her professional counterparts. A voracious reader of the latest books and articles and a tireless attendee at conferences, she endlessly drops off Xerox copies of handouts in mail boxes with the intimidating note, "Here's what's coming down the pike," or sends emails identifying dozens of sources and links that require immediate follow-up if we are to remain "with it."

Sheila epitomizes the Internet and blogging. She outgoogles Google. Her drive is to find the best that is, adapt it to fit, scale it so that it is absorbable, and present it on a platter as a customized deliverable. No small or mean feat because that involves a savvy knowledge of organizational structure and company implementation routes.

What she offers is a kind of package deal not accompanied by any internal depth analysis or diagnostics except that justified by what others have found, what they are doing with success, and what therefore can accrue to us. The problems and problem-solving processes identified and endorsed are whatever are the current preoccupations of the industry and business analysts. And when new solutions appear on the horizon, she is quick to offer the more current replacement back-up. As savvy survivors, evolution is our mantra and adaptation our salvation.

Clearly, the Sheilas are preferable to the Mikes. At least we are not driving forward by looking in the rearview mirror. To be sure, her total championing of the new is often oppressive and undifferentiated. She herself is not a researcher; nor does she call for such originality in-house or require it of herself. Her exclusive strategy is to run the company's nightly news program and to be consoled by its regular presentation of reality. But such truth telling may embody a number of major shortcomings or tradeoffs.

The external becomes not only a substitute for the internal, but also the inside is systematically emptied to the point where all that remains is an operating top of Sheilas and an adjunct force of order takers. Outsourcing becomes the ultimate model of total adaptation. But imitation is not innovation. Although dizzying in number, choice is still determining; those driven by currency are typically short term, which may preclude later positioning. Above all, the quick and multiples fixes to ensure immediate survival fall short of the unique survival power of discovery—that every genuine breakthrough is potentially a new business, a new lease on life for your company, or, if ignored and taken up by others, the thing that could put you out of business. Finally, excessive adaptation and absorption in the present may lure and seal you off from a future that in fact is the preserve of innovation alone.

The Innovator—Permanent Transition

Rachel has not come to her present fascination and embrace of innovation overnight. Indeed, she has passed through being both a Mike and a Sheila and is thus better able not only to understand and value their contributions but also to be aware of how formidable and deflective they can be. Above all, what has steadied her focus and singled her out is a series of constant questions beginning always with "Yes, but," progressing to "I am not so sure that is the answer," and finally wondering out loud whether "the emperor has no clothes."

The first and recurrent threshold of innovation is thus problem uncertainty. What confronts us is not so clear or resolvable as the Sheilas would have us believe. The issue is often not in focus but rather blurred at the edges. Its center is busy and shifting and eludes easy or rapid classification. Its current diagnosis seems glib and enjoys a momentum of agreement that may be deceptively persuasive. So-called second opinions lose their value when they turn out to be largely and obediently confirmatory. What makes the case for Sheila makes the more reflective Rachel uneasy. She begins to note that neither the problem statement nor the solution is total or inclusive; major parts are left out or over. Could it be, Rachel wonders, that what we see is not really what is—that it is not only the proverbial tip of the iceberg but also not typically found in these waters? Suddenly, Sheila's flashy fashioning gives way and has less hold as Rachel begins to ask of the problem whether its erratic behavior is characteristic of the playful antics of the Artful Dodger or of Tricky Dickie. Occasionally, mythological nomenclature is invoked to grant it formidable recurrency. Does it behave in mercurial or chameleon-like fashion like Proteus or is it an overreacher like Prometheus? But what ultimately persuades and attracts Rachel is that none of the standard processes are able to tame or classify the beast.

But even that stage of qualifying the problem is not enough. Rachel has to determine whether investing the problem with sufficient intransigence justifies its being granted the centrality of innovation. Rachel wants to make sure at the outset that pursuing this problem is worth her time and focus—that, although elusive, it is not a will o' the wisp; its tantalizing tip has no depth to it, and it ultimately will be perceived as a transparent enigma. The qualifying tests of the next stage take the various forms used often to test trends and typically not applied by or to the Sheilas. Does the problem appear to possess durability or is it temporary? An awkward transition that will be replaced by the return of cyclical stability? Will its ability to last be accompanied by continued impact and discontinuity? And if it gives way, does it embryonically contain its successor? Is this transition to be followed by a return to equilibrium or by a new transition, until transition not stability becomes the norm? Curiously classifying an enigma as recurrently aberrational clinches for Rachel its status as an innovative problem requiring an innovative solution. It also now becomes Rachel's characteristic choice as the defining driver of her professional identity.

Although Rachel still has far to go on her journey to innovation with no guarantees of success, what overall conclusions if any can be drawn at this point? The first and perhaps most obvious is the importance of problem triage. The question of whether all should subsequently be offered innovation instruction should not obscure the need for such minimum, across-the-board triage discrimination training. Equally as important is its application to organizational differentiation. Problem profiling sets up professional profiling. Each of the three has to be granted their place given the sorting out of problem definitions.

But the dilemma that often occurs is that of exclusivity—where each one claims it alone possesses the keys to heaven and seeks to drum out or dominate the others. Giving problems their separate due is to be followed by allowing and affirming professionals to make and honor their various choices and apply their craft.

Mike and all the other adapters of the tried and the true need to be given their heads and process 80 percent of what is going on. The company thus remains operationally sound and continues to generate income. The Sheilas and all the appliers are invaluable reminders that more is changing than remaining the same and that the question of what the competition is doing needs now to include what the research shows. But an absolute commitment to currency serves at best as a threshold for innovation but stops short of embracing its disturbing discontinuity.

Rachel and other innovators not only choose and define one-of-a-kind problems but also do so with yields that normalize aberration. Indeed, the overall effect of granting each group its value and function is that collectively they may increase the visibility, importance, and difference of innovation and thereby compete to attract new recruits to their ranks. But perhaps the most unexpected outcome is the linkage of innovation and leadership.

Minimally, three leadership options surface. The first is the recognition that the overall orchestration of and coexistence of all professional types requires the balance and balancing acts of leadership. But that does not preclude the leadership initiative of assigning company priority to innovation, serving as its advocate and running interference, and pressuring HR to redefine and find the best and the brightest as the most skeptical disturbers of the peace.

Finally, although many leaders are not innovators themselves, they can nevertheless harvest its many benefits. They can position their leadership and organization at the intersect of present and the future. They thereby can hearken to the leadership messages that innovation is the key to the future and foretells of where we should be going and what smart choices we should be making. CEOs who do not fully embrace innovation's future are more followers than leaders and lead companies that lose their lead. Innovation leaders live the future, which is the principal reason they are often misunderstood and not followed. They offer stretch, not shock, and enlightenment, not desperation, as the midwives of a new future, ones that introduce us to circular thinking.

Circular Problem Solving 28

A CLASSIC FORMULATION OF THE problem-solving process involves three stages: know-what, know-how, and know-why. The first involves tapping the knowledge of what one knows. The second brings to bear what one has learned from the applications of such knowledge. Finally, the last draws upon the systemic knowledge of how things and people interact to solve problems and to implement solutions.

That all sounds so sensible and logical. But at least three concerns surface:

1. Sequence. One can argue that the last should really go first. Problem solving should be not only methodological but also thoughtful and conceptual. It should also be an interactive thinking and learning experience. If know-why were first, learning would join thinking from the outset. The two would constantly task each other and in the process raise the level of both, as well as the quality of the solution. In short, the questions asked and in what order determines whether the problem-solving process is progressive or circular (single or double loop).

2. Hidden drama of interplay. Typically, the problem solver remains removed and apart from the problem. He is the subject examining an object. But he does not question or

examine how his methodological approach or even perception of the problem may contribute and alter the object. He would not hesitate to call for more data or information if needed but hardly ever pauses to reflect on what he and his method unknowingly may bring to the process. Indeed, the need for know-why may not only be in the wrong order but also need to be applied both to the problem and to the problem solver.

3. Fit. There is no one problem-solving system. A number of factors determine selection. Often the choice of one proceeds from the recognition that there are different orders of complexity, as well as levels of expectations on both the problem and solution side. Goals also determine choice. It makes an enormous difference whether the objective is improvement or innovation. Finally, the organizational culture plays a key role in favoring and shaping the preferred problem solving mode. GE always and only uses Six Sigma.

Regardless of approach, what is clear is that problem solving is perhaps the most dominant and dominating activity of the entire workforce from top to bottom. Indeed, how one solves may be how one succeeds. According to anthropologists, that it is also how cultures think, learn, and ultimately lead. In short, knowing where to place know-why determines whether the thinking, learning, and leading trinity is progressive or circular, whether it leads to greater understanding and adaptability, and finally whether it confers the ultimate gift of innovation. Happily, multiple intelligence (MI) nicely complicates and enriches both progressive and circular problem solving.

Progressive Process

Progressive problem solving is linear-sequential; that is, it goes forward in a straight and tight series of incremental steps or gains. It is thus always additive. It is a series of statements not questions. It reflects the use of a singular intelligence. It is always a checklist. Here is how it marshals data and information to move through its essential stages:

Know-What
1. Raw Data (unlabeled and without direction) (know-what)
2. Data Categorized (now designated and ordered)
3. Data Formatted (now is information)

Know-How
4. Information Applied (now knowledge)

Know-Why
5. Knowledge Applied (problem solved)

Circular and Multiple Process

The circular does not abandon the linear-sequential but encloses it. It also not only begins with know-why but uses that question as its constant spearhead and prod. Three specific areas are brought into play: data (know-what), methodology, and end goals.

Thus, the first three steps above now are multiplied and become subject to five questions:

- What do we know?
- What don't we know?
- What don't we know we don't know?
- What is enough to know to problem solve?
- What can we learn that we did not know from the process itself?

Next, methodology multiply perceived is folded into the inquiry process:

- What kind of thinking shapes our characteristic problem-solving mode?
- What assumptions do we bring to the problem that may require its being redefined or repositioned?
- What can be learned or discovered that can be built into the problem-solving process?

Finally, end goals as drivers and assessment:

- Have we got it right given the goals?
- Have we got it as right as we can get it?
- Have we simulated? Can it live, thrive, and function in real time, with real people, in a real world?

- Does the solution have a future?
- Does the problem have a greater future than the solution?

Of course, not all problems are complicated and need to be multiply approached. Many are pretty straightforward and can be solved quickly and progressively. But the argument here is that much of what is new and discontinuous has left its mark on the emergence of new and disconcerting problems.

1. More and more of current problems are of a different, more contrary, and intractable nature. As such they are not as amenable to the conventional, fast, progressive mode, although that may not stop its knee-jerk adoption.
2. Information technology tracking is now more dynamic. It exists in real time and in just-in-time. It is more instructive and renders processes transparent and accessible while they are in motion. The analogy in the medical field is going from MRIs to fMRIs. The latter records and measures brain activity in response to a variety of different kinds of questions asked. Such data flow and tracking now increasingly eludes the calipers of progressive problem solving.
3. The ante has been upped from continuous improvement to continuous innovation. Once a different future and innovation enter and drive the scheme of things, standard problem solving is not enough. What is needed is more— more multiple, more circular, more holistic thinking, learning, and leading. One creative source of such enrichment and amplification is multiple intelligence.

Innovation is always more busy than still, more a motion picture than a series of snapshots. Process trumps product; the journey is always superior to arrival; know-why ultimately drives know-how. The genius of the Deming-Japanese partnership was not quality— that was only its defining sign—but innovation. The achievement was an unwavering commitment to continuous improvement as continuous innovation. Everything was grist for the mill, especially the obvious. And worker comfort and intelligence were as much objects for improvement as quality-driven products and services. In short, to ensure that quality was not an add-on applied at the end of the assembly line, innovation was to be distributed, embedded, and practiced throughout the entire process. Indeed, innovation became the overarching guide of the process itself.

The obvious solution of copying the Japanese, which many have tried, generally has failed. The reasons for the lack of easy transference, however, are instructive, for they also define the three major obstacles and issues confronting all innovation training:

1. *Organization.* A commitment to innovation cannot be superficial or partial. Rather, it compels a total change in company culture, mission, and structure. Specifically, it requires the creation of an environment receptive to the discontinuity of creativity. It also requires an innovation leader.
2. *Training.* Can creativity even be taught? Or is it like leadership—inborn, not acquired? Then, too, how does it fit in with current program training? Does it displace the current focus on productivity? The relationship between innovation and all other training is part and parcel of working out the larger relationship between innovation and productivity.
3. *Workforce and Management.* What is the innovation capacity of employees? Should creativity training be available across the board? With what costs? And what about generating expectations that may be disappointed?

Although the emphasis here is on the last point, innovation training, if it is not to be stillborn, ultimately requires bringing together and converging the other two dimensions of the challenge. Indeed, much of the formidable nature of developing innovation training derives from its obvious and hidden entanglements with organizational structures and training capacity.

An examination of post-WWII literature and practices of creativity, as well as the various ways it has been assessed and taught in the past, reveals a mixed bag of operating assumptions:

1. Everyone has the potential for creativity.
2. Innovation can be taught.

3. No one approach works.
4. Multiplicity rules.
5. Generally, innovation eludes assessment.

Did the training of innovation work? It stirred the pot, shook things up, was often fun, but generally did not produce results commensurate with the investment or its grandiose claims sufficient to ensure continuance. Above all, the rigors of ROI were never included in the evaluation equation. Although there are many reasons for both its popularity and demise, the principal one is that it was not needy enough.

Competition was not as intense as it is now, and productivity was not a survival goal. There was little insistence on a more explicit and urgent linkage of innovation to business objectives. The other problem was obsessive guru focus. All eggs were put in one basket—in the brilliant concepts and exercises of an Edward de Bono, for example—who violated some of his own commandments. Finally, not unlike its distance from practical applications, innovation as a cognitive faculty was generally isolated and enjoyed star status. Thus, it was not linked to its kinship faculties that could ensure wider application and access to diverse learning styles and modes.

Nevertheless, the five assumptions above constitute a workable starting point to guide current and future innovation training. But they need to be extended with the following supplements:

6. Existing instruments for assessing innovation capacity are valid and still can be used. (Myers-Briggs, after all, classifies kinds of thinking.)
7. Developing new tests for innovation may have to wait and be informed by the findings of brain research, cognitive psychology, and genetic studies.
8. Across-the-board innovation training must yield wider company results if it is to be justified.
9. Innovation thus has to be linked to the ways we think, our modes of inquiry, and finally the rich diversity of learning pathways.
10. Innovation training is threshold training.

But innovation does not occur without advocates and enthusiasts.

Innovation Advocates, Enthusiasts, and Evangelists

29

T HE NEW AND THE YOUNG RESEMBLE each other: both are heady, assertive, and arrogant. Both seek to be free of origins and history, to exist independently, on their own, without any debts or obligations to continuity. Enormously powerful, innovation can end old businesses, create new ones, impart new life to current ones—any or all of the above at any or all times. The old dilemma of how to stir such creative upstarts is thus compounded by the fear that it will be an ingrate and bite the hand that feeds it. Innovative outcomes are thus always a mix of new starts and end-games. But acknowledging and managing such ambiguity is not a familiar operating assumption of traditional leadership.

Who then are the principal supporters of innovation? And equally as important, why? There are minimally three kinds of leaders, and they differ and vary in degree of intensity.

Advocates of the New

The first are the CEO advocates of the new. They know what innovation can do for their bottom line, morale, and organizational unity. Innovation is almost a fix that they need to keep going and to preserve corporate identity. It is the critical means to all survival and growth ends. No purists here; these leaders accept every version they can get.

They particularly encourage all incremental advances: variations of ingredients or amounts of familiar formulas; any tweaks that reduce costs; any shortcuts that involve less time; any packaging arrangement that grants another look. Of course they would also welcome the genuinely creative and disruptive, which creates new markets and brands. But they view such exceptions as ideals that are hard to rely on and come by. Better thus to settle for what is at a lower level and easier to generate. In short, to these leaders, innovation is really marketing and advertising. All real creativity is invested in packaging and selling the new.

The Enthusiasts

Next are the enthusiasts. As CEOs they typically traffic in visions. They invoke the glories of what once was as benchmarks of what can be again. Often cheerleaders, they call upon all to rise to the new occasion of saving the company by regaining its previous leadership position and market share.

But despite the passion and slogans, they are not so much genuine leaders as users of innovation. They know its power to lift and inspire, to stir the juices, and to promise salvation. They also know its carrying capacity to weather storms and to get through hard times. Their visions are thus more political and tactical but do not possess or speak from a knowledgeable core of creativity.

Typically they surround themselves with "me too" people. Like the CEO, they have run out of growth options and reluctantly been backed into the creativity corner. They are neither comfortable nor happy being there; they do not number innovative types among their friends or associates; and they confess almost proudly that they do not have a creative bone in their body. If members of the executive team, they believe they have to support the CEO. They generally do not submit any minority reports. They exhibit alignment so absolute and demanding that they are all obedient echoes. Whatever differences they may have are subdued by the triumph of chain of command. In any case, unity rules, and innovation for better or worse is the unifier. The current situation is so desperate that it requires putting all our eggs in the creativity basket and searching for the magic bullet.

The Evangelists

Finally, there are the true believers, the evangelists. These leaders are authentic. They have been creative in their own right, understand the reluctance and hang-ups of artistic temperaments, and are aware of how difficult it is to coax and manage emerging innovators. Above all, they value what the creation of an innovative culture can do for a company over and above whatever it may create. They understand its power to attract and keep talent and what it means to work in an environment that is alive and constantly curious and to work with associates who are restless energizers. But above all, these leaders have some ideas of how to make that culture happen—and, even more importantly, of what it is linked to.

Minimally, innovation is sustained by five factors:

1. First, it is linked to vision of the big new idea. Indeed, by inhabiting the same ground as the CEO, creativity minimally and persuasively reinforces the focus on vision.
2. Second, it is systemic. Innovation can lead the charge because it is macro-worthy—it inhabits the Parthenon.
3. It crosses the line—into the future. It thus invites the journey of unity of common commitment and thereby the potential of serving as an inclusive company culture.
4. Innovation is ideological. It is the epitome of transformation. As such, it is emblematic of change for all.
5. Finally, it supports a new kind of leadership that argues for a partnership between the incremental and the disruptive and introduces such doubleness as a twenty-first-century training norm.

A double argument thus emerges: to identify the forces that traditionally and recurrently shape and reshape vision, on the one hand, and then to introduce and position innovation as the central driver of this brave new worldview, on the other. Thus from the outset the beginnings and ends of creativity have to be linked to the same ambiguous interplay of such similar agents of vision. In addition, innovation and vision so paired cannot be ordered or commanded to emerge. They have to be coached, even teased out. Their commonality indeed should come as a surprise. In short, it is the outcome not of action but of reflection—of stepping back, pausing, and taking in the whole—and then visioning the forces of origins and ends.

Such shaping of a new big picture thus should not be deliverable, already predigested or predetermined, but an exploration of what is seminal and recurrent. Trainers thus have to develop exploratory models of vision and innovation. The initial one would be led by and for the executive team. Then it would be adapted for general workforce application. A special adaptation would then become the orientation program for new hires. What would be the content? Although the essentials of vision vary, its basic components always possess the recurrent and classic nature and behaviors of archetypes. The following five, it can be argued, have both the resiliency and pliability to be constant, yet redefinable, and to sustain the illustrative examples that accompany each one: the new idea, systems, foresight, ideology, and leadership.

The New Idea!

Ideas are still civilization's most powerful mind-altering drug. Whether used as a lens to see the world in a new light or as an instance of discovery and insight—"I have an idea!"—big ideas not only shape the big picture but also contain embryonically their yet-to-be discovered versions. Conceptual nominations can range from the new globality, in which the world is of a piece economically and ecologically or is now a flat and endlessly proliferating network or both.

But in all instances the test is the power of re-conception to see doubly—to bridge the then with the now, and the now with the future. By seeking to close if not eliminate the gap between continuity and change, ideas function as the eternal version of the work in progress.

Systems

Systems are secrets connected by purpose. Although their patterns of meaning and relationship typically may operate beneath the surface even at great depth, when discovered, displayed, and tracked, they prove to be startlingly verifiable and unifying. The focus of archetypal system inquiry is thus always two-fold. First, can all that is emerging fit in and be absorbed by existing paradigms? Or can such organizing systems be revised or redefined to facilitate accommodation? Failing that, are there new systems or ecologies that have the maternal inclusiveness to accept and mother a new brood of those who do not look alike and are contentiously independent? But lest the nominating process be indulgent, all new or redefined archetypes must be systemic.

Foresight

Although looking ahead should be common to all archetypal inquiry, for foresight to be genuine and brave it must abandon the predictability of extrapolation and systematically focus instead on the disruptive. What's new must give way to what's next. In other words, strategic planners have to not only become futurists but also embrace both that profession's reading and techniques of the laws and behaviors of discontinuous futures. Such anticipatory specialists over five decades have developed the expertise to see the future as a transparent enigma worthy of archetypal status.

Ideology

All forecasts are three-fold. They identify the probable (most likely), the possible (including wild cards), and the preferable (what is hoped for). It is the last that offers the prospect or illusion of control and purpose and that always has constituted the ideology of archetypes. The mediation between traditional and new values thus is potentially directive and promises the exoneration of justification. But, as with all reviewed and redefined archetypes, the outcomes must be totally inclusive, capable of diverse consensus, and futuristically sustainable.

In other words, ideology of all considerations invokes and applies its parallel partners to discipline its own quest. Otherwise ideology will render all aspiration as partisan and based on exclusivity. My keys to heaven should not lock you out.

Leadership

Who is in charge and who decisively chooses what future to pursue is critical. It must avoid at the outset the danger of archetypes becoming stereotypes. The future chosen must be imaged as itself innovative—incarnate so that they become one when fleshed or born. Not unexpectedly, that cutting edge exists at the periphery. The future that emerges is coincidental with upstarts and start-ups. Innovation emerges initially as a minority voice disturbing the universe.

The process of birth involves a number of transformations: imagining the unfamiliar, then imagining the unimaginable, then imagining the unimaginable as the familiar, and then managing the unmanageable. In the process, it has to structure the emergence of the future, but one that offers the comfort of at least a familiar alien from outer space.

Happily, a new version of CEO evangelism has appeared, which is helpful in that it structures further the nature of leadership innovation intelligence. The new rallying cry from CEOs is "Make mistakes!" At least that is what Proctor & Gamble's former CEO A.G. Lafley urged and, to make sure we get the message, a table is provided, titled "A.G. Lafley's 11 Biggest Innovation 'Failures.'"

Of course, the moment such errors are embraced, personalized, and bear your name, wisdom and humility walk hand in hand. Actually, Lafley's advice is not new. Not too long ago, Richard Farson enshrined the same concept in more paradoxical terms: "The Success of Failure, the Failure of Success." Shortly thereafter, Gary Hamel warned us about risk-averse CEOs and managers whose timidity may jeopardize both the current and the future bottom line. Finally, another broadside was directed recently against complacent executives living off past capital by Mark Gottfredson and Steve Schaubert in *The Breakthrough Imperative* (2008).

What is going on? Why this preoccupation with a conscious commitment to error? The conviction that failure is the absolute path to creative success? But is it always and infallibly? And even if error is the threshold of creativity, how do we un-program a generation of overachievers and teach them how to stumble? And finally while we wait for this paradox to generate wonders, what do we do in the meantime? Hold our breaths and hope for the redemption of a failed innovation?

Hardly—innovation leadership puts together a more sensible and imaginative set of initiatives to manage and stir the ongoing, the sudden breakthrough, and the way ahead. Here are at least three initiatives that leaders might launch in tandem that span the range of hedging bets and playing wild cards.

The Ongoing Mainstream—The Now

Failure aversion is not necessarily a bad thing, our innovative enthusiasts notwithstanding. Many of our most productive managers cannot handle or manage error, and they shouldn't have to. In a few cases, it would drive them crazy.

In our craze for the eureka moment, let us not overlook the strong and steady commitment to continuous improvement and the constant tweaking that generates incremental gains in products and services quality. In other words, don't quit your day job. Let us not throw out the every day baby of productivity for the heady waters of creativity. The business has to go on. It cannot be put on hold while the brain trust burns the midnight oil. Besides, you could not find a more exacting group to test the latest innovations than those who have successfully been working out the bugs and turning a sow's ear into a purse for many years. The mainstream still remains the ultimate reality check.

Tangential Breakthrough Teams—The Emerging

Search out those professionals with a high tolerance for paradox, ambiguity, and speculation—especially if they tend to be loners, a little ornery, and hard to get along with. Group them by their differences: disciplines, units, degrees, age, gender, nationality, and so forth. Create as many teams, even, or especially, if they overlap; ideally, all should be impressed by themselves, think they are da Vinci's gift to the world, and miniaturize the whole. Suggest unfamiliar places where they can meet, but never during regular work hours or days.

Their agenda? Compile what is crazy. Make it clear that it cannot be incremental or familiar. The ultimate test is that it must be a start-up—able to begin in a garage and spawn a completely new business, especially one that is life-threatening, one that, if we don't create or adopt it, will put us out of business. Nothing will be monitored or evaluated; no one will review the list. Every two weeks it is to send any artifacts, drawings, or miniatures to the CEO and one other of one's choice.

The CEO Seminar on the Future of the Future—The Innovative

While all this is going on, the executive team has to pull its collective head out of operations and become stargazers. Every two weeks they are to play leapfrog; while we are catching up, let us also get ahead of the pack. Nothing is out of bounds. The range of the meetings should be 360 degrees, the scope global, and the topic or approach somewhat radical. Invite wild cards, an occasional end-of-world type, gurus on innovations, and even a few far-out pontificating academics. The unifying subject is what's new, but fused with what's ahead; it should have the durability of a mega-trend. The test of discontinuity is that every vice president should leave with a different scenario of creation in his head than what he came in with and should perhaps begin to have different dreams.

Will it all work? In a sense it has to. It spans the now, the emerging, and the brand new; it differentiates between the everyday doers, the off-the-wall creative types, and the big picture and policy-making chiefs at the helm. Will innovation occur? Undoubtedly. The only questions are these: How long will it take for the lone rangers to collaborate creatively? What increases in innovation productivity will occur over time? And finally, how fast can the mainstream wire the new in place so as to become industry leaders?

Meanwhile, the stargazers will continue to prepare the agenda for the next decade while those celebrating failure have made an enemy of the future.

SOME FINAL WORRIES, WARNINGS, AND WISDOMS

IV

CEOs—You Don't Want to Make an Enemy of the Future! 30

WHAT AN ODD WARNING! WE have always regarded the future as a friend—an enabler that helped us to solve and parcel out problems too big and demanding to manage solely in the present. Or it offered a tabula rasa for new starts or visions—a way of reinventing ourselves. Or, failing that, the future was at least neutral—a level playing field. But an adversary? Even an enemy? That's new—disturbing. What is going on? Why is looking ahead so dangerous, especially now?

Are we also claiming that this twenty-first-century future is different from all past futures—that it is less familiar, more unfriendly, and even hostile to the plans and aspirations of leaders and managers? If so, then what sets this future apart? There are at least five threats.

It Is Knowable

Typically the challenge was unpredictability. That got our juices flowing. Strategy always included Plan B. Hedging our bets was standard risk management. Executive intuition often came to the rescue. But a future that is already known? That is like playing with a marked deck—it makes no difference because you lose in either case. In short, we are not used to managing loss, including loss of leadership as a future game.

Less Tolerant

There is generally less margin for error—less play in the bottom line. We can't afford any or too many mistakes. Stakes are too high. All is precarious; one miscalculation can put you out of business. Costs have to be reined in. Every decision has to be perfect—every implementation flawless—every executive team a brilliant think tank.

Scaled Up

What used to be macro is now global. We don't know where we are in this new order or who will be our competitors, where they will come from, what they are capable of, and how they can madden us with cost differentials so low that the comforting advantage of distance disappears. We are thus always being surprised—caught off guard desperately trying to find a predictable pattern for apparently random, non-reoccurring singular events.

We are in the new catch-up game of trying to get our bearings in this global system and, in the process, beginning to acknowledge reluctantly that it may be synonymous with this new, unfriendly future. Reschedule your next executive retreat, and include a number of international stops where you can search for adaptive versions of the new global model.

Capitalism Reconsidered?

Free enterprise and trade assume bounty. Scarcity is entertained primarily as a cost factor of supply and demand. But when resources are not only limited but also finite—and when haves and have nots squabble over the same necessities—then economic systems may have to move toward a new dynamic of future relationships between entrepreneurship and state planning. The days of the lone ranger and going it alone may be over. The future may have to become a trust fund held in common. It may be time for emergence of the CEO-statesman.

Future Smarts

This future needs to be moved into the present, where it can coexist with all current operations and serve as the backdrop against which we play out all strategic decisions. We have to become more expert at understanding how this different future behaves and misbehaves and how to make it work for us. We may have to join the World Future Society, attend its professional meetings, and add its bibliography to our leadership library. Above all, we may have to reposition and accept the future as our ultimate measure—our future evaluator.

But why can't we cope? For at least three reasons. First, we have more information than we know what to do with. Then, too, much of it is incoherent—unconnected, unintegrated, and often even conflictive data. Second, on top of that, members of the executive team are often from the same generation, mount their favorite hobbyhorses, and press forward with their chorus of future warnings, worries, and wisdoms. Office politics and jockeying, which at this critical point should probably be muted, regularly rear their partisan heads and revolve around a new version of whose ox is gored—namely, whose voice and view has most access to the executive ear. And, finally, strategic planners echoing members of the board call for taking care of current short-term business problems as the version of the longer term—for both present, and not just future, viability. So what are leaders and managers to do? Where should they turn? One suggestion is to develop and apply diagnostic scenarios.

What is that? It is a fusion methodology. From the outset it puts together problem solving and forecasting and decision-making with its projected reverberating impacts—solution and positioning. In short, it facilitates leapfrogging; while we are catching up and taking care of present business, let us also try to get ahead. It also functions as a screening process: identifying and defining those problems and decisions that are not familiar or run of the mill but strike terror into a CEO's heart because they imperil survival and because they are in bed with a discontinuous future. What's involved? Minimally, there are five steps.

Problem Sharing

Who else has this problem (of talent shortages, profit margins, global competition, etc.)? What have they projected as its future impacts? What is its extent? Industry-specific or does it cross sectors? Regional, national, global? Is any company immune?

In other words, is there anyone who does not have this problem? Finally is the problem like the proverbial iceberg—bigger and more entangling and hidden than we thought? And is it solvable—once and for all—or will it continue to plague us for years to come?

Future Scaling

Did we ever have this problem before? And, if solved, was it linked to a particular future that in effect shaped, eased, and welcomed its solution? Or are you claiming that this is a new problem and that it is secretly connected to the troublesome future it points to? That can't be. There is nothing new under the sun. Check the index of all the leadership books; it has to be there in one form or another. Or is this a paradigm shift of paradigm shifts? And are we already at that intersect? Is the world really flat after all?

Future Fusions

Take both the problem and our business on a time journey. Develop three scenarios—one predictable, one terrible, and one wild card. Dump the problem in each. What happens? Do we survive, grow, or disappear? Is the problem still around but we are not? Above all, does the problem have a future? Does it persist? Is it tenacious, long term? Or has it morphed before our eyes into something else—a lovely butterfly of opportunity or the menacing shape of a hostile acquisition or merger? If we are still around—in the same business—what do we look like? Above all, am I still around?

Globalizing Contexts

Are there different cultural, nationalistic, or even ideological ways of solving the problem and projecting the future? How would the French, Germans, and Russians go about it? The Japanese, Chinese, the Indians? Do they each have different futures that make their problem-solving processes more effective, less timid, more long term?

Are we prisoners of our short-term quarterly fixation to such an extent that it determines not only our focus but also our inability to fuse problem and future solving? Suppose we were to outsource or subcontract our problem to the Danes or the Chinese—what would be the result? Would it be better than what we come up with? Would they also have difficulties? But not the same ones? Are we stuck in our traditional strengths?

Innovation: Future-Driven Solutions

The ultimate end result of diagnostic scenarios is creative exhaustion. All the tried and true strategies turn out to be tired and jaded platitudes, our standard visions fail to engage and even pale before a future that does not welcome us, we experience the throwback of being a start-up, and in desperation we hear the familiar call: think outside the box. Piece by piece the problem-solving and visioning toolbox is emptied and we find ourselves not *in media res* but at genesis—not being asked to add another chapter but to craft a new creation story.

Diagnostic scenarios thus minimally offer three gifts. First, the methodology defines the new box we are in so that we don't reproduce or take it with us when we change vantage points. Second, it signals cross-roads, paradigm shifts, and the imperative of innovation. Third, it develops the ultimate test for defining innovation as the creation of a new business that never existed before. The final vision posed then is to become or incorporate that new venture, armed now with the knowledge gained by diagnostic scenarios that, if we don't, someone else will and in the process perhaps put us out of business.

In America we now sadly are preoccupied with endgames and losing the lead. We therefore need new tools, MBA programs, and executive teams to fuse problem solving and strategic planning, to bridge and manage discontinuity, to recover our future, and to support leaders who use diagnostic scenarios to make innovation the bottom line of the future and shape the look of leaders to come.

Never Minimize Contexts: The Dynamics of Five Future Leadership Models

U NCERTAINTY HAS MADE IT MORE difficult to attract out-standing candidates to fill the projected executive openings and often even more confusing to do so; still, when the dust has settled, five major leadership models emerge that are discernible and durable. The first two, transformational and transactional, are based on traditional models with variations; one variation seeks an enlargement of that leadership role, the other a contraction. The third or middle position of innovator supports distributed, not singular, leadership. It follows a multiple management model in which various individuals, more or less equal, singly, collectively, and collaboratively are creative. The fourth and fifth options, anticipatory and converger, like the first two are also variations on each other and exhibit the same emphasis of arguing for more or less.

In all, then, three dynamics are involved. The first involves the intense interactive traffic that constantly takes place between these five types over time. The second marks the sudden emergence of singular amalgams or hybrids that uniquely, albeit temporally, fill the breech. Finally, least recognized and acknowledged is the battleground where the clash of the titans takes place: special contexts shaped, defined, and spawned by their own hybriding. Clearly, it would be remiss not to examine those contexts and their roles as final determiners of why hybrids are in fact the mode of our age.

Leadership Expanded

Those championing the expansion of the role of the leader argue that it is required to ensure reform. The leader has to be become supreme. That role is the key to improving performance and accountability. But the problem is every administrator is limited by the range of his own expert subject matter. The more the leader expands his instructional range, the more he crosses over into areas beyond his knowledge; it is at those points that the audience may withdraw and question whether he knows what he is talking about.

In part this has led to distributed leadership, redefined in this case as distributed subject-matter competencies. The leader had to stop short of claiming generic subject-matter competence and instead share, in a distributed fashion, with those who held the various competencies, the leadership of the whole.

Leadership Contracted

The second model in fact picks up precisely at this point. It is time perhaps that we stop insisting that all CEOs be both super-leaders and super-micro-managers. Indeed, the job should be defined in such a way that few will want the job and even fewer may be effective in it. Particularly sad are the number of leaders who exhibit the classic hubris of displaying an excessive pride in their martyred exhaustion. Unless we limit the range and the focus of the leader, we will lose the opportunity to attract, train, and retain a new generation of leaders for the twenty-first century.

Leadership Distributed

The concern was that the increasing complexity and verticality of large major corporations was distancing employees from the decision-making process. That was particularly lamentable because they had a great deal to contribute. Specifically, research discovered a link between participatory decision-making and innovation. In effect, then, a double gain was being offered.

Servant-leadership required employees to be involved so that leaders do not believe that they are indispensable and enjoy a monopoly on leadership. High on the list was the persuasive competence of employees to provide the CEO with the means to become a servant-leader. The litmus test of that role taking hold would be the transfer of leadership from the CEO to the organization.

Convergence compels the recognition that leadership is not in fact the sole perogative of the CEO. Rather, it is available to and from everyone in the organization. Some have written it into employee job descriptions. Distributed leadership reinforces the role of the leader to "develop everyone you touch." The value of distributed leadership is leveling the vertical to the horizontal. That way the collective and collaborative task of administering is diffused across the board. At the same time, the issue of generic knowledge is muted as subject-matter competence is now in the hands of those who already possessed it. Distributed leadership is not a recasting of committees where workers make recommendations to the almighty vertical god, but a genuinely horizontal and participatory collaborative. But the key is the willingness of the leader to be less than the total authority, to share not just responsibility but also power, and to endow each worker with a participatory role in decision-making.

This far more empowering version of site-based management requires the CEO to accept the new role of the servant-leader. However, with many posing as martyrs, few may be willing to give up or share their stigmata. Under the aegis of distributed leadership, an organization increasingly becomes cooperative, collective, and collaborative. The vertical pyramid is leveled horizontally. Hopefully, what emerges over time is an innovative and futuristic system that is a leader in the field. In addition, distributed leadership in effect has forced to the forefront a question that up until now has not been even posed before: Who shall lead? What shall be the leadership configurations of the future?

The increased burdens imposed on leadership, the bifurcated structures of management and metrics as at odds with each other, and the general incapacity of a number of current administrators to achieve real proximity to and leverage on teacher development and student achievement as a unified and reciprocal focus has created a vacuum that worker-manager teachers in large part and for the first time alone are filling.

Leadership Partnered

Curiously, the fourth model derives its impetus and strength from a response to the problem of the intellectual limitations of one leader being able to be 360 degrees and to command comprehensive subject-matter competence. Not being even first among equals on the team, in fact, the group says, "We're all leaders." The CEO's role is now non-invasive. He prods and stimulates the administrative team to make informed and optimum decisions, factors in as the voice of the customer, and shares business perceptions. Finally—and here is where the issue of instructional leadership joins the case—he serves as an advocate for a triangle linkage: development, achievement, and best practices.

Before exploring the last model of leadership, it might be helpful to pause and identify some of the typical ways we think about the future and how to manage it. Typically, we want the present to become the future. That is reassuring and preserves continuity. Thus, what drives, to different degrees and in various ways, all four models surveyed so far is the necessity to preserve leadership itself. Consider the following urgent calls:

1. The CEO needs to do more, particularly in providing instructional leadership. Therefore, let us help him expand his role as an academic leader.
2. The leader needs to do less, especially if he is to provide instructional leadership. Therefore, let us find ways to relieve him of his business and managerial duties.
3. But in both cases the CEO needs to establish subject-matter credibility. Therefore, we need to develop a new definition of subject-matter competence as leadership content as knowledge literacy.
4. The leadership needs to be extended horizontally so that it is distributed rather than concentrated. That also will solve the problem of the limited range of subject-matter competence and acceptance.

Trust can guide benign abandonment: teams can be empowered to run things. The CEO moves from the center to the periphery. He becomes a broker, an internal consultant, an executive team coach—a guide on the side rather than a star on the stage.

Throughout, preserving leadership in one form or another is still the focus. But is there a next step where all these models in fact may be leading us? That of the worker-leader, which may have the capacity to be even superior to the conventional single leader in all his variations.

Learning-Led Organizations

Worker-led companies existed earlier as the vision or metaphor of a number of researchers who believed, if business could embrace leadership as a meaningful option, it would do much to reposition business in the twenty-first century. To appreciate its difference as a model from the others, it may be helpful to list its main governance distinctions:

1. Workers alone provide leadership. There are no bosses.
2. They remain workers.
3. They are not identified as administrators and thus do not require state or district certification.
4. They are learning leaders, each in charge of a team responsible for a cohort of no more than one hundred. Scale provides coherence and community; small is always better than big. The number of learning leaders needed would be determined by the population and its operating structure.
5. Each learning leader would be assisted by a collaborative team who would service the cohort.
6. The business side of the house would be handled by a business manager whose task it would be to facilitate goals and not create financial fiefdoms of beauracratic impotence. Some functions would be outsourced.
7. Cost controls would be a collective team responsibility. Budgets may not be exceeded. Any surpluses remain with the team and may be carried over to the next operating year.
8. Evaluation would take the form of 360-degree assessments, which would factor in high-stakes testing but not be the only, or even the primary, source of evaluation.

9. Appointment of learning leaders requires team worker approval. They serve three-year renewable terms. They are paid at least 30 percent more than the highest-paid vice president. New members of the learning team are hired and fired by the team.

10. Learning leaders are removable or renewable by a majority of the members of the team.

11. Learning leaders of all cohorts constitute the learning leader council to establish company goals, priorities, policies, and procedures. Elected representatives from this group make up the district-wide council.

12. Finally, and most important of all, the mission of each learning team is to provide for the integration of administration, instruction, and measurement (AIM). That way administration and measurement are intimate and proximate to instruction, feedback is constant and immediate, diagnostics and interventions follow on the heels of each other, and students centered by 360-degree assessment and teachers by a similar holistic structure are involved in a seamless and transparent process.

Would it work? It already has. In effect it is the next step in the evolution of delivering distributed collaborative education. Leadership would be transferred directly to the workforce. No elaborate intermediary structure or roles would be needed because they would have been internalized within a new collaborative unit, which simultaneously administers, teaches, and measures the effectiveness of achievement.

Will it be adopted by others? Perhaps as a last resort. If enough are persuaded that tinkering with the first two models of leadership takes care of the problem, that model will remain the dominant solution. Sadly, many workers for the most part will probably not support worker leadership. The prospect of not having a paternal figure strikes terror in their hearts. Only about 25 percent would be willing to become leaders. Nor would the unions, whom one might believe would happily embrace the cause, do so. They have developed a number of relationships with the existing administrative hierarchies that are too comfortable for them to become adventuresome. Even boards who are accustomed to the clarity of finding fault with administrators would not be happy to confront a host of worker-leaders. Obviously, the various associations of professional administrators will resist the idea of such leaders to the death.

So what is the upshot? Are we tilting at windmills? The argument comes down to this: administrative partnerships, with or without CEOs, should represent and be preceived as a respectable minority option. As such, there is the need to provide the separate visibility and viability of an alternative. Such an option also needs to be held up by serious advocates of reform to those who will be filling current and future vacancies. There is even the possibility of attracting professionals who ordinarily might not consider entering the ring.

Specifically, such alternatives may attract administrative candidates open to partnering and distributed leadership, and receptive to becoming worker leaders. Equally as important, these alternatives must be put before colleges, so that they might begin to prepare managers for being leaders without becoming administrators, and administrators for being leaders without being lone rangers.

Above all, we have to preserve the prospect that we may be describing a new future norm and that the current minority position may in fact become a dominant one. If in fact that occurs, then the current discussion follows the dynamics of leapfrogging—while we are catching up, let us also seek to get ahead. The future houses all the alternatives. Hybrids embrace them all.

CPSIA information can be obtained at www.ICGtesting.com
Printed in the USA
269827BV00002B/1/P